THE
FUR-TRADE FLEET

THE
FUR-TRADE FLEET
Shipwrecks of the Hudson's Bay Company

ANTHONY DALTON

VICTORIA · VANCOUVER · CALGARY

Heritage House Publishing Company Ltd.
www.heritagehouse.ca

Library and Archives Canada Cataloguing in Publication
Dalton, Anthony, 1940–
  The fur-trade fleet : shipwrecks of the Hudson's Bay Company / Anthony Dalton.

(Amazing stories)
Includes bibliographical references and index.
Issued also in electronic format.
ISBN 978-1-926936-09-3

  1. Shipwrecks—Arctic regions—History-20th century. 2. Hudson's Bay Company—History—20th century. 3. Fur trade—Canada—History-20th century. 4. Arctic regions—History—20th century. I. Title. II. Series: Amazing stories (Surrey, B.C.)

G525.D34 2011   910.9163'27   C2011-900350-3

Series editor: Lesley Reynolds.
Cover design: Chyla Cardinal. Interior design: Frances Hunter.
Cover photo: RMS *Nascopie* on a Cape Dorset reef in 1947 (HBC Archives/Archives of Manitoba 1987/363-N-8D).

The interior of this book was printed on 100% post-consumer recycled paper, processed chlorine free and printed with vegetable-based inks.

Heritage House acknowledges the financial support for its publishing program from the Government of Canada through the Canada Book Fund (CBF), Canada Council for the Arts and the province of British Columbia through the British Columbia Arts Council and the Book Publishing Tax Credit.

14 13 12 11 1 2 3 4 5
Printed in Canada

To my cousins:
Barbara Ridley, Brian Corby and Alan Corby

Your father introduced me to the sea when I was a boy. Without being aware of it, he helped me embark on a lifelong voyage to explore the world.

This book is for him, and for you.

Contents

Prologue

CAPTAIN THOMAS SMELLIE WAS NERVOUS, *although he kept his feelings from his crew. He paced the bridge, his hands deep in the pockets of his duffle coat, his eyes roaming the waters ahead and to each side. Off to port, the Labrador coast was visible in the early evening light. To starboard, a series of islands dotted the view. The sea was calm with only a slight swell rolling in from the vast Atlantic Ocean.*

Captain Smellie was not completely happy with his ship. He had been with her since her difficult launching at Ardrossan, Scotland, in the spring of 1926. They had completed one voyage together, travelling along this same coastline and into Hudson Bay the year before. So far, on this second northern voyage, they had steamed from Montreal to Cartwright, Labrador, and on to Hopedale without mishap. Still, the captain was worried. SS Bayrupert was loaded with supplies, which meant her draft was at least 24 feet. That was a lot of ship below the waterline. Much of the Labrador coast was uncharted; no one knew where the next underwater obstruction might be.

Nain was to be the next port of call. Captain Smellie would have taken a smaller ship closer in to reduce steaming time, but Bayrupert was a different matter. He decided to get more sea room and pass the scattered islands at a distance. Just past the Farmyard Islands, he took Bayrupert 15 miles out to sea. From there he turned to port and steamed north, planning to correct his course when due east of Nain and then run straight in to the anchorage.

The captain had been on the bridge most of the night. At 7:00 a.m., sure that the ship now had more than enough salt water between her keel and the seabed, he handed over command of the bridge to the first officer and went to his cabin for a rest. As always, he left instructions to be called immediately in the event of a problem.

Not far ahead, and in a direct line with the approaching ship, an uncharted pinnacle of sheer rock pierced the water, rising from the sea bottom to stand like a submerged sentry, its head 22 feet below the surface.

Bayrupert rolled easily with the swells, making a vague corkscrew motion as she moved from side to side and fore and aft. It was the kind of rhythm that sailors adjust to and stop noticing after a while. Captain Smellie stretched out on his bunk fully dressed and closed his eyes.

Prologue

Ten minutes after the captain left the bridge, *Bayrupert's* bow lifted in the air, as it had been doing repeatedly since the ship left the islands. It ploughed into a trough on the way down, sending a torrent of spray over the foredeck. Another swell raised her again, holding her high for a few seconds. As the bow dropped into the next trough between the swells, the ship crunched down on something hard and stopped dead in the water.

Introduction

WITHOUT THE ATTRACTION OF THE beaver and its extraordinary pelt, the Company of Adventurers might never have existed. By extension, without the group of influential Englishmen who called themselves the Company of Adventurers, the Hudson's Bay Company (HBC) would not have been established, and Canada, as we know it, might be quite different.

The beaver is a fascinating creature that is often incorrectly considered to be uniquely Canadian. It is, of course, widely recognized as Canada's national emblem, but beavers were once common in Europe and across Asia to China until excessive hunting reduced these populations to dangerously low levels. The same would eventually happen in

North America. The once-ubiquitous beaver, second-largest rodent in the world and the largest in North America, was the main focus of HBC endeavours.

Beavers live in shallow river valleys bordered by trees, where they can control the water levels for their own protection against other creatures—all except man, for beavers are easy to trap. In addition to their valuable furs, they also have scent glands that secrete castoreum, which is used in the manufacture of perfume.

It has been said that King Solomon, the wise monarch of ancient Israel, wore beaver skins. If so, it was an unusual choice for a ruler when so many other heads of nations chose more exotic furs from lions, leopards, the beautiful sable antelopes, or bears.

Two Frenchmen, Pierre-Esprit Radisson and his partner, Médard Chouart, Sieur des Groseilliers, are credited with opening royal British eyes to the lucrative possibilities of the fur trade in North America and the potential value of beaver pelts. Thanks to Radisson and Groseilliers, the king's cousin, Prince Rupert of the Rhine, took an interest in forming a syndicate to fund an expedition to Hudson Bay for the express purpose of trading for furs and searching for precious metals, such as gold, silver and copper.

When the tiny *Nonsuch* sailed from Gravesend, on the south bank of England's Thames River, in June 1668, she was accompanied by the chartered ketch *Eaglet*. The two impossibly small sailing ships were bound across the

North Atlantic, up the Davis Strait, through Hudson Strait and deep into Hudson Bay on an historic fur-trading mission. Commissioned by Prince Rupert and his co-investors in the newly formed Company of Adventurers, the forerunner of the HBC, the instructions to the two captains began thus: "You are with the first wind that presents to saile with the sd. Vessel unto Hudsons Bay either by the Northward or Westward according to your owne discretion endeavouring to keepe company as much as you can and in order there unto you are to appointe your Places of rendezvous in case of separation."

Once out on the North Atlantic, however, *Eaglet* was unable to keep station with *Nonsuch*. A storm separated the two ships, and *Eaglet* almost became the first casualty of the future HBC. It is to her captain's credit that he and his crew were able to work the damaged ketch back to an English port. *Nonsuch* continued alone and completed her exploratory trading voyage to Hudson Bay. After enduring a bitterly cold winter in a homemade fort on a river's mouth in James Bay, she returned to England in the summer of 1669 laden with furs and with her crew intact. *Nonsuch* never made another voyage for the Company of Adventurers or the HBC, but she did earn her way into the history books. She also contributed in a significant measure to the craze for beaver hats.

Nonsuch was a mere 53 feet long and weighed in at only 100 tons. She was followed over the next 300 years by a vast fleet of sailing ships, motor vessels and steamers. Most of them were hundreds of tons larger than the ketch that helped build the HBC. They entered countless ports and harbours on the Pacific coast, the east coast and the coasts of Hudson Bay and probed deep into uncharted Arctic waters. Considering the vast number of voyages made by HBC ships and the conditions under which they operated, it is perhaps surprising that there were relatively few losses. For example, a report in the Hudson's Bay Company Archives in Winnipeg notes that there were 664 round-trip voyages made between British ports and Hudson Bay during the 243 years from 1670 to 1913. The report does not state how many ships were involved in those hundreds of voyages, only that 21 were wrecked either in the bay or in Hudson Strait. A further seven were badly damaged, presumably by contact with ice. Considering the large number of voyages and the dangers involved, that's not a bad record.

1

The Battle on the Bay

THE HBC GOVERNORS IN LONDON were first and foremost businessmen, sending their merchant ships into Hudson Bay to trade and to bring back bales of valuable furs. They were not interested in getting into a fight with anyone, especially a foreign power. A war on Hudson Bay, which the British considered their rightful territory, was a potential disaster for a commercial enterprise. The French, however, who had been in the North American fur trade longer than the British, were envious of the profits the HBC trading posts were making on Hudson Bay, and they wanted to do something about it.

The obvious solution, at least to Jacques-René de Brisay, Marquis de Denonville, the governor of New France (Quebec), was to send an overland party of just over 100 men to capture

the HBC posts. It was an inspired idea that proved successful from the outset. Leaving Montreal in March 1686, using
sleds and canoes, the French war party covered the difficult 800 miles of untracked snow-covered ground to Moose
Factory, at the foot of James Bay, in just 82 days. The attackers
were led by two French-Canadian brothers, Pierre Le Moyne
d'Iberville and Jacques Le Moyne de Sainte-Hélène, under
the command of the Chevalier Pierre de Troyes.

It took only a couple of hours to overwhelm the 16 men
in the Moose Factory HBC fort. The next target was Rupert
House, 75 miles up the coast. Leaving less than half their
number to hold Moose Factory, the victorious but now-
depleted French force paddled north in a fleet of canoes
and took their second post without any more trouble than
the first. Along with the fort, they also took charge of the
cannons. An added bonus was the HBC's small supply ship
Craven, which stood at anchor just offshore. D'Iberville captured the vessel and used it to attack the next post on de
Troyes' wish list: Fort Albany.

De Troyes and d'Iberville were on a roll and took Albany
without a real fight. They had hauled the cannons with them
and bombarded the fort's palisades with 140 rounds of heavy
shot to demoralize the inhabitants. Faced with the possibility of
the destruction of their home and workplace, the HBC personnel surrendered. De Troyes and a contingent of men trekked
back to Quebec. D'Iberville had to spend the winter on Hudson
Bay, doing very little apart from maintaining French ownership

of the three captured forts. By the end of winter he was bored and ready for action again. First, though, he had to take care of his prizes. Getting all the bales of captured furs away from the three forts and transporting them to France posed a problem: D'Iberville did not have a ship big enough to cross the Atlantic. To solve this problem, he marched back to Quebec and booked passage on a ship for France. There he took command of a frigate with the distinctly non-northern name of *Soleil d'Afrique* (African Sun) and sailed back to Hudson Bay.

Meanwhile, the English had not taken the outrage lightly. Although they were traditional enemies, England and France were not technically at war with each other at the time. In London, the HBC's governing body was determined to get its forts and furs back. They immediately dispatched two warships and 85 men to recapture Albany and teach the upstart Frenchmen a lesson. So confident were they of success that they also sent Captain John Marsh, a new governor, and William Bond, the recently appointed admiral of the HBC. Bond was, in fact, the first and only admiral employed by the company. D'Iberville was already in the bay by this time, busy loading bales of furs from a base on Charlton Island. He was in the act of leaving for Albany with the furs loaded on a small sloop for transport to *Soleil d'Afrique*, when *Churchill*, carrying 18 guns, and an accompanying frigate, *Yonge*, hove into view. Although he was outnumbered four to one, d'Iberville had no intention of relinquishing his prizes, and he proved that he was no fool.

He sent some of his men out in canoes to strip the channel markers from the Albany River, causing the two warships to run aground. They were refloated later, but the Frenchman had made his point. He had won the first round. The English moored their ships to an island in sight of the fort and set up camp. The siege of Fort Albany had begun, but the French quickly took control of the situation.

D'Iberville used snipers to keep the English confined to the island and, therefore, unable to hunt for fresh meat or find other food. The new governor never did have a chance to govern his domain—he died of scurvy before the next summer arrived. Admiral William Bond was captured with a party of men when he tried to go hunting. To complete the demoralization of the English force, d'Iberville pounded their camp with cannon shot from a nearby bluff until they surrendered. Again, he had won the battle. A few months later, when the weather improved, d'Iberville sailed away with the additional English ships loaded with prisoners and the furs.

The Montreal-born Frenchman was back on the bay again in 1690 with three different ships. By this time, England and France really were at war with each other. Ever ambitious and determined to take over all the HBC's holdings on the shores of Hudson Bay, d'Iberville anchored his ships at Five Fathom Hole, just outside the mouth of the Hayes River and in sight of the important HBC post of York Factory. This time, though, he had a bit of a surprise. An English man-of-war, carrying 36 heavy guns, stood guard over York Factory.

D'Iberville was nothing if not resilient. He changed his plans, hauled anchors and sailed southeast to Fort Severn, which he captured along with its stock of furs. Once again, he left the bay in triumph.

The English, understandably, became tired of the Frenchman's persecutions. Two years after Fort Severn fell, they dispatched a strong force of three HBC frigates and a fire ship. On board, in addition to 82 guns and the ships' crews, were 213 marines with rifles. In command was James Knight, a company man through and through. A former shipwright from Deptford, south London, who had worked for the HBC since 1676, he had energy and mental agility in abundance. Within six years of joining the HBC as a carpenter, he had risen to the post of chief factor at Fort Albany. Knight's first order of business would be to recapture his old post. He did so without much trouble and was rewarded by the repossession of 30,000 beaver pelts from the storeroom.

The determined d'Iberville refused to give up. He sailed back to York Factory for another attempt at capturing the fort in 1694. This time, he and his small shipboard army overwhelmed the untrained defenders of York Factory. D'Iberville renamed the important post Fort Bourbon, left a contingent of men in charge and sailed off to France with all the furs he could find. Leaving the fort, however, was not a good idea. The following year, the Royal Navy came calling with three well-armed frigates and took it away from the French again.

HMS *Hampshire* fights with Pierre Le Moyne d'Iberville's *Pélican* at close quarters during the 1697 Battle on the Bay.

HBC ARCHIVES/ARCHIVES OF MANITOBA P-401

Despite that setback, d'Iberville again proved that he was not easily discouraged. In 1697, when King Louis XIV asked him to go back to Hudson Bay and take over as many of the English fur-trading posts as possible, he accepted the job immediately. Four ships left France and sailed in convoy as far as Hudson Strait. There they found the route west blocked by thick ice. D'Iberville's flagship, the 44-gun *Pélican*, managed to get free of the ice and into the bay. Rather than wait for his other three ships, d'Iberville set course for the Hayes River and anchored at Five Fathom Hole within sight of York Factory. While some of his men were ashore, a lookout spotted sails approaching from the north. Three ships soon appeared, and d'Iberville assumed they were the rest of his convoy.

By the time d'Iberville realized his mistake, three English ships were upon him. He didn't hesitate. Although he was desperately short-handed, and one ship against three, he prepared to fight, and fight he did.

The three English ships consisted of two owned by the HBC and one Royal Navy frigate chartered to look after them. HMS *Hampshire*, the 52-gun navy frigate, was under the command of Captain John Fletcher. The other two ships were the HBC's 32-gun frigate *Royal Hudson's Bay* and the armed freighter *Dering*. A fourth HBC ship, *Owner's Love*, sailing in convoy with them from England, had been lost in the ice of Hudson Strait on the way to the bay.

The ensuing four-hour battle must have been spectacular to watch. *Pélican* breezed past *Hampshire* under full sail and with all guns on that side firing. *Hampshire* retaliated with an accurate broadside that reduced *Pélican*'s sails and rigging to shreds. *Royal Hudson's Bay* and *Dering* joined in, raking the French ship's deck with grapeshot and small-arms fire. *Dering* also managed to score a devastating direct hit on *Pélican*'s prow, tearing it off in the process.

Hampshire's captain, John Fletcher, called on d'Iberville to surrender. The Frenchman refused. The two ships were fighting so close that the men on board could see each other clearly. In a magnificent gesture, Fletcher raised a glass of wine to his opponent's courage. D'Iberville returned the salute in a like manner before resuming the battle.

Outnumbered, outgunned, severely damaged but far from beaten, *Pélican* slammed a broadside into *Hampshire* at close range, hitting the English frigate along the waterline. That was the end of *Hampshire*. She drifted onto a shoal and sank, taking all hands with her. Wasting no time, *Pélican* turned her guns on *Royal Hudson's Bay*, forcing her crew to surrender. Soon after, taking advantage of a sudden squall, *Dering* fled for the sanctuary of the Nelson River. The storm blew *Royal Hudson's Bay* into shallow water where she settled to the bottom. All the men aboard—the crew and some of the French invaders—were able to get to land.

The sea battle was over, but *Pélican*, the victor, had suffered too much damage to survive. The powerful storm winds drove the shattered ship onto a sandbar. The crew had to swim for the distant shore, holding on to whatever wreckage they could find. Some made it, but at least 18 men drowned, adding their number to those lost in the battle.

An artist's fanciful rendition of the sinking of *Pélican* after she had defeated three HBC ships off the mouth of the Hayes River in 1697.
WIKIMEDIA COMMONS

France had won the Battle on the Bay, but the English still held York Factory, and the very much alive d'Iberville wanted it for France. Once again, fate played into his hands: the missing French ships arrived. D'Iberville and his surviving sailors attacked York Factory from the land, while the newcomers attacked from the sea. York Factory fell under the onslaught when Henry Bayley, the chief factor, decided to surrender.

Winter was fast approaching. The French ships loaded up with furs and, with the valiant Pierre Le Moyne d'Iberville aboard, set sail for France. His work was done; he had fulfilled his king's commission. D'Iberville would never return to Hudson Bay. This time, the French managed to hold on to York Factory for 16 years, until the Treaty of Utrecht handed it back to the English, in the guise of the HBC.

CHAPTER

2

James Knight's
Last Voyage

ADVENTURERS AND MERCHANTS BEGAN TO explore
Hudson Bay in the early 17th century. The ill-fated Henry
Hudson, who gave his name and his life to the vast inland
sea, sailed to the southernmost reaches of James Bay,
which extends from the south end of Hudson Bay. In 1631,
another Englishman, Captain Luke Foxe, in command of
the 70-ton ex-naval vessel *Charles*, was the first to probe
into the bay's northwest extremity and explore the body of
ice and water now known as Foxe Basin, located between
the west coast of Baffin Island and the east coast of the
Melville Peninsula. Foxe was in charge of an expedition
searching for the Northwest Passage. He was unsuccessful due to the ice concentration, but instead of sailing for

26

home, he changed direction and explored farther south along the west side of Hudson Bay. Foxe reported sailing through upwards of 40 whales near a small group of islands. One of these islands was, he thought, worthy of special mention. He wrote of coming up to "a low island all of white marble." As far as we know, Foxe was the first European to see or land on Marble Island.

Marble Island stands 24 miles offshore from the modern settlement of Rankin Inlet on the west coast of Hudson Bay, a few miles south of Chesterfield Inlet. A narrow natural harbour separates Marble Island from the smaller Quartzite Island. The islands of rounded hills ground smooth by glacial activity are bleak but have a stark beauty.

Marble Island has long been noted for walrus herds, polar bears and occasional whales—bowheads and belugas in particular. It is also notorious for inclement weather and heavy ice for much of every year. Apart from its natural wonders, it is a sacred site for the Inuit. In Native folklore, the island is the spiritual home of an old Inuit woman who remained behind onshore when the rest of her family moved to a new land where the hunting was better. The old woman looked out to sea and noticed that the ice appeared to represent an island. She made a wish that the ice would turn into a real island so she could live there. When her family came back two years later, there was no sign of the old woman, but they heard her voice telling them, "My spirit lives on this marble island."

Ever since then, without exception, when the Inuit go ashore on Marble Island they do so on their knees out of respect for the old woman's memory. Inuit legend tells that anyone who fails to crawl ashore from their boat will suffer great misfortune within one year. One explicit version of the legend warns that those who do not crawl ashore will die *exactly* one year to the day later.

In 1719, Marble Island and Quartzite Island were the morbid setting for a tragedy that befell the crews of two British ships. It is a story that would not be fully exposed for over 270 years.

James Knight was a rough and tough local governor of the HBC with many years experience in the bay. He had beaten the French to recapture Fort Albany in 1693 and had governed the posts at York Factory and at Churchill. During his tenure at York Factory, Knight befriended a Chipewyan girl named Thanadelthur. She had been captured and enslaved by the Crees but escaped and found her way to the HBC fort on the Hayes River. Knight had been having difficulty setting up a trading agreement with the Chipewyans, who were afraid of the well-armed Crees who lived between them and the fort. He recognized Thanadelthur's intelligence and value as an interpreter and sent her on a mission to persuade the Chipewyans to make peace with the Crees and come to the fort to trade. After a difficult journey of adventure and misadventure, she was eventually successful.

Thanadelthur told Knight stories of substantial mineral deposits where a northern river ran into the Arctic sea. Knight became convinced that this river could well be the link that would join Hudson Bay with the open sea to China. It appeared to him that the river could be a route through the mythical and as yet undiscovered Northwest Passage—with the added attraction of potential riches from the precious metals he believed would be found on the way.

Excited by the possibility, Knight returned to England to convince his superiors in the HBC that, with their approval and backing, he could successfully navigate through the North and reach China and all the treasures it offered. His appeal must have been eloquent and passionate, because even though he was almost certainly in his early seventies, his plan was accepted.

In June 1719, James Knight and his crews, which numbered somewhere from 26 to 40 men, depending on the report, set sail from Gravesend in two ships: the 80-ton frigate *Albany* and the 40-ton sloop *Discovery*. Well aware of the possibility of being separated at sea, the captains agreed that if the two ships lost each other in the North Atlantic, they were to meet in the vicinity of Resolution Island, on the north side of the eastern end of Hudson Strait. From there, and in convoy, they would explore the coast of Hudson Bay north of Churchill and along the east shore of the Melville Peninsula on Foxe Basin. Their goal was to sail as far north as possible, preferably beyond the 69th parallel, and find the opening to the Northwest Passage, at that time often referred to as the Strait of Anian.

Knight could not have known it, but he was, in a sense, on the right track. There is a potential sea route through the Arctic from Foxe Basin, although it is of no real use to shipping. Fury and Hecla Strait connects Foxe Basin with the Gulf of Boothia and, at the top of Boothia Peninsula, with Bellot Strait. The short and narrow Bellot Strait is usually ice choked and has a formidable current. It is, however, part of the Northwest Passage between Prince Regent Inlet and Franklin Strait. In order to reach Bellot Strait from Foxe Basin without circumnavigating most of Baffin Island, ships must go through Fury and Hecla Strait, which was unknown to Europeans and therefore unnamed by them in Knight's time, as was Bellot Strait. Fury and Hecla Strait is over 100 miles long and up to 15 miles wide. Like Bellot Strait, it has a strong west-to-east current and is rarely free of heavy ice. Knight's two ships could never have passed through Fury and Hecla Strait, even if they had been able to force their way through the ice of Foxe Basin to find the entrance.

Knight's two expedition ships sailed across the Atlantic, through Hudson Strait and into Hudson Bay, although no one in England had definitive proof of that for over four decades. *Albany* and *Discovery* simply sailed away from England and disappeared. We can be sure the expedition reached the west coast of Hudson Bay, somewhere north of

Churchill. Based on later discoveries, it is most likely that the two ships were caught in a storm and driven up onto the smooth, rocky shores of either Marble Island or nearby Quartzite Island. Both ships were wrecked, and the survivors among the crew set up camp on Marble Island, perhaps without crawling to safety on hands and knees as Inuit legend required. The theory of the storm as a cause of the wreck is conjecture, but it is the most likely possibility.

No concrete evidence of either ship or their crews was found until two years later. The HBC's boy explorer, Henry Kelsey, landed on Marble Island and found the remains of a shipwreck. The next year, another HBC captain, John Scroggs, sailing north along the same coast, found additional wreckage on the island, and his crew heard tales from Natives of a lone man who sat on one of the islands looking out to sea—to the south. It was far from conclusive proof of the fate of the Knight expedition, but despite that lack, Scroggs made no attempt to search further for stronger evidence. He sent a report to the HBC that both of Knight's ships had sunk and surmised that the crews had been murdered by Natives. That report, based on guesswork, effectively closed the book on James Knight for the time being.

Another 43 years passed. In 1765, the HBC made a first attempt at whaling in the Marble Island region. Although this hunt was not successful, it did pave the way for other visitors. Two years later, a crew from the HBC whaling ship *Success* found a stone building, said to be Knight's house. They also found a large amount of coal and a few graves. Local Natives suggested that some of the crew members of the two long-missing ships managed to survive the first winter, but they did not know what happened to them after that. Presumably the man reported earlier was one of the survivors.

The legendary Samuel Hearne followed soon after in the sloop *Churchill*, also owned by the HBC. Upon hearing the stories, Hearne went ashore on Marble Island to look at the finds. At that time, he also saw the remains of two ships lay-ing in five fathoms of water. Hearne, a careful explorer, had found the missing remnants of the Knight expedition.

Hearne went back to Marble Island each summer for the next two years. On one occasion, he found *Albany*'s fig-urehead and a few more remnants from the wrecks, which he sent to London as proof of the disaster. He also claimed to have talked with Inuit elders and gradually learned what he was convinced was the true story of the disaster. Hearne said the Inuit told him that the expedition ships arrived at Marble Island in the fall of 1719. The story is skimpy on detail, and some elements are almost certainly fiction, but it does give a reasonable representation of what could have happened, except that it ignores one obvious fact. *Albany*, the story says, was badly damaged while entering the narrow harbour. Trapped on the island, the sailors died of "sickness and famine." One wonders where the sloop *Discovery* and her crew were at the time.

In fact, the remains of both ships are on the seabed close to each other in the natural harbour between Marble Island and Quartzite Island, where Hearne said he saw them. They were examined by divers from a scientific expedition in 1990. The most likely conclusion remains that *Albany* and *Discovery* were wrecked in a storm and sank together between the islands. The officers and crews surely knew that they were within a few days travel from Churchill, but whether they reached the mainland or stayed on the islands, they all died before reaching safety. The disappearance of James Knight and his men created a mystery that may never be fully solved.

3

In Peril
on Hudson Bay

THE HBC SAILING SHIP *Happy Return* did not live up to her optimistic name. Under the command of Captain William Bond, she was lost in Hudson Strait in the summer of 1686 while en route from England to the James Bay trading posts. Drifting ice and little-understood sea currents almost certainly played a part in *Happy Return*'s demise.

The HBC sent its sailing ships to follow the difficult routes through Hudson Strait and into Hudson Bay each navigable season. In their reports, especially those made public, the company suggested that few ships made the voyage because the straits were difficult to navigate. American and British whaling ships sailed through Hudson Strait for the whaling grounds of Hudson Bay each summer for much of the 18th and 19th centuries. The accounts of Hudson Strait recorded by American whalers, in particular, differ from the HBC's version, as does the account of Joseph Robson, who spent six years on the west side of the bay in the 18th century. During that time, he lived at York Factory for a while and also at Churchill. Robson wrote, "As the Straits, then, are never frozen over, nor always unnavigable, even when there is much ice in the Bay, I imagine that a safe passage may be found in the beginning of June." Robson also wrote that ships could leave York Factory in early November and still get out of the bay and through the straits before freeze-up.

That might well have been true in some years, but not always. Despite what whalers and others said or wrote, Hudson Strait was a dangerous place at any time for a ship, especially one powered only by sails. The HBC Archives and most fur-trade historians maintain that 13 HBC ships were wrecked in Hudson Bay. That number does not include others that suffered substantial damage but were saved by their crews, or those that were wrecked in Hudson Strait.

The Company of Adventurers chartered a three-masted pink from the Royal Navy in 1670. Pinks were flat-bottomed sailing ships with three masts. They developed unpleasant rolling characteristics in heavy seas, yet many made successful transoceanic voyages. *Wivenhoe*, the chartered pink, was about the same size as *Nonsuch*. She sailed in company with the much larger *Prince Rupert*. On August 19, 1670, *Wivenhoe* almost came to grief on the rocks near Mansel Island on the northeast side of Hudson Bay. Less than a month later, on September 14, she ran aground in thick fog off Port Nelson but was taken off without damage and returned to England the following year. *Wivenhoe* survived Hudson Bay; many more ships owned or chartered by the company did not.

In 1680, Captain Richard Greenway sailed from Charlton Island in the 140-ton wooden sailing ship *Prudent Mary*. She was loaded with furs and bound for faraway England. Fifteen miles north of Charlton Island, *Prudent Mary* ran up on a reef off Trodely Island. Although the ship was lost, most of the cargo was salvaged, and captain and crew survived to make their way to the safety of Fort Albany.

Captain Zachariah Gillam, who had piloted *Nonsuch* on her successful 1668 voyage, lost his life in Hudson Bay in 1682. He was then captain of the wooden frigate *Prince Rupert* (the first of eight HBC sailing ships with that name). The ship was anchored in the Nelson River with only the captain and nine crew aboard (the rest of the crew and a few passengers being ashore), when drifting ice caused her to drag her anchor and drift out into the bay. There, the ice ruptured her hull and sent the elegant sailing ship and all aboard her to the seabed.

Three years after *Prudent Mary* was wrecked, her first mate, Richard Lucas, sailed back to the bay on a trading voyage in command of a small wooden ketch aptly named

Expectation. It was believed that Lucas had hidden some of *Prudent Mary*'s cargo and was intending to retrieve it. Captain Nehemiah Walker of the HBC captured *Expectation* and was taking her to the company fort at Moose Factory when he wrecked her on Charlton Island in 1683.

The wooden frigate *Pery* (or possibly *Perry*) ran aground in the Albany River near Fort Albany in September 1711. Despite Captain Richard Ward's efforts, the ship sank in the river, although the crew were able to salvage some of her cargo.

In August 1724, another wooden frigate, *Mary (I)*, was homeward bound for England from southern James Bay with passengers and a cargo of furs when she ran up on Weston Island, 35 miles due north of Charlton Island. The ship and cargo were lost, but all passengers and crew made the difficult crossing to Fort Albany in the ship's boats and spent a harsh winter there, instead of in their warm homes in England.

Ice wrecked the wooden brigantine *Esquimaux* in October 1836. She was a supply ship sailing out of London each year to posts in Hudson and James bays. On the short voyage from York Factory to Churchill, she encountered heavy ice and thick fog. Her rudder froze, and she drifted with the ice in an easterly direction, instead of sailing north as planned. She sank four miles off Cape Tatnam.

Another brigantine, the flush-decked *Eagle,* became stranded on Button Island in late 1836 and had to spend the winter in the Hayes River. A year later, after leaving Fort Chimo en route for England, she was found to be taking in two inches of water every hour. The HBC sold her because she was not worth repairing.

Two years after *Eagle* wintered in the Hayes River, a chartered wooden sailing ship, *Effort*, was en route from York Factory, at the mouth of the Hayes River, to Montreal when she disappeared. It is possible that she fetched up on the Belcher Islands and was wrecked, while her crew, according to Inuit legend, were murdered there by Natives.

On August 13th, 1864, *Prince Arthur* and *Prince of Wales* piled up on Mansel Island within an hour of each other. Mansel Island is in the northeast extremity of the bay, where it joins Hudson Strait. Historian Charles Napier Bell wrote of a Moose Factory resident who commented on the accidents to the two ships:

> Both of these really fine vessels went ashore one lovely moonlight night at 10 o'clock. The weather was beautiful at the time and the ships were carrying studding sails allow and aloft on both sides. A few hours previous to the accident the captains of the respective vessels had been interchanging visits, the sea being quite calm, sufficiently so at any rate for ship's boats. They were close to the island, consequently should have known danger. No lives were lost and a great portion of the cargoes was saved.

Prince of Wales was recovered and repaired enough to make port. There are two widely varying reports of what happened. One states that *Prince of Wales*'s crew took off the wrecked *Prince Arthur*'s crew and cargo; the other holds that *Prince of Wales* was wrecked as well, and the crews of both ships were taken home on *Ocean Nymph*. In fact, both ships did run up on Mansel Island.

The majority of the HBC's sailing ships were built in Britain. One of the exceptions was the 340-ton brigantine *Cam Owen*. A product of Grand River, Prince Edward Island, in 1883, *Cam Owen* sailed under the command of Captain John Hawes with a crew of 13 men. *Cam Owen* made her final voyage to Hudson Bay in 1886. She was wrecked at the end of August when, almost within sight of Churchill, a gale slammed into her. Captain Hawes and his crew worked hard to keep the ship off the shore, but the gale forced her into the land near Cape Churchill. She soon began taking on more water than the pumps could handle, making any attempt to sail away from the coast a suicidal exercise. Hawes took the only option possible. In a desperate bid to save the lives of his passengers and crew, he ran *Cam Owen* ashore at high tide about 20 miles south of Cape Churchill.

Captain Hawes was lucky that night. The tide rose a full eight feet higher than normal, allowing him to take his ship over the reefs and settle her on the beach—damaged, but with all on board alive and well. When the tide ebbed, the passengers and crew were able to clamber off the ship and walk to solid ground. One of the officers and a couple of men took a small boat along the coast to Churchill for help. They returned with two local boats and a handful of landsmen, hoping to salvage at least some of the much-needed supplies.

Although it was still summer, ice was already forming along the shore, adding to the hazards. When the rescue party arrived at the scene, they found everyone safe and camped onshore. *Cam Owen*, however, was a wreck. If the tide had not been so abnormally high, she would surely have foundered on one of the reefs offshore. There was little that could be done to salvage the cargo, although some supplies were taken off. The ship was almost submerged at high tide and encased in a thin film of ice as she emerged with the outgoing tide. Some time later, the ice carried her away to a private burial at sea.

One of the most beautiful ships in the HBC fleet was the 583-ton brigantine *Princess Royal. Princess* was built in 1853 and sent to the west coast of North America in June 1854. For the next 30 years, she made regular round-trip voyages to west coast ports. In 1885, she made her first and only voyage to Hudson Bay. After unloading supplies and taking on furs, she left Moose Factory late in the season, her captain hoping to get clear of the bay before winter ice came in. His hopes were dashed when he ran into a thick snowstorm while heading north to get out of James Bay. With no room to manoeuvre, the captain had two anchors run out, with 75 fathoms of chain on each. *Princess Royal* rode the storm for 20 hours before the wind and waves combined to part the chains. The ship was driven back to the sandbar off Moose Island, where she hit hard and broke her back.

There were more wrecks to come. Eighteen years later, another series of reports reached the HBC headquarters in London, all to do with another of the company's three-masted ships gone to the bottom. One letter was sent on September 30, 1903, to the commissioner of the HBC in Winnipeg from the sub-collector of Canada Customs at Moose Factory. In the letter, which arrived on October 27, the official stated, "I regret having to report that the Lady Head was stranded on the Gasket Shoal on the 17th. Inst. & was abandoned by the crew on the 25th in a sinking condition." Another ship lost; another valuable cargo gone to the seabed.

James Bay is littered with islands and shoals, many of which were uncharted in the early years of the 20th century. Gasket Shoal is a typical example. It is a tiny, semi-submerged rocky islet, roughly 26 miles southeast of the southeast corner of Akimiski Island, the largest piece of land in James Bay.

The weather in James Bay in September of 1903 was atrocious. The three-masted barque *Lady Head* was not the only vessel in trouble. A separate report from Moose Factory, also sent on September 30, noted, "The Albany barge & SS Chipman were driven ashore during a severe gale." In this instance, both were saved, as were their cargoes. The writer ended his report with, "I may add that the gales & weather generally that has prevailed in the Bay this fall is something unprecedented."

The elegant three-masted barque *Lady Head* served Hudson Bay posts until she was wrecked on Gasket Shoal in September 1903.
HBC ARCHIVES/ARCHIVES OF MANITOBA 1987/363-L-8/3

Captain John G. Ford, master of *Lady Head*, wrote that he sailed from the depot on Charlton Island on September 15. The 457-ton ship was bound for England, carrying a cargo of furs with an estimated value at the time of almost $288,000, plus the value of "sundry packages, chronometer, etc." The weather was foggy with a northeast wind as the ship beat her way north, the crew taking soundings with a lead at regular intervals. The last sounding taken on the evening of September 17 gave a depth of 14 fathoms. *Lady Head* struck Gasket Shoal 45 minutes later. Due to the rolling seas, her hull ground on the rocks, creating more damage with each strike. In addition to her cargo of furs, *Lady Head* was loaded with stone ballast. To lighten her and reduce her draft, the crew off-loaded "between 30 & 40 Tons of stone," and the ship floated free on September 21.

For the safety of the ship and all on board, Captain Ford had two anchors run out with 60 fathoms of chain, while his crew manned the pumps and worked hard to repair their ship. The weather played false again, the wind veering to strike from the northwest and rapidly building to gale force. *Lady Head* shook her three masts and cross-trees, straining at the anchorage. The wind pushed and pulled at her, bending her to its will. The anchors and chain began to drag, and the gale forced the ship onto Gasket Shoal for a second time. *Lady Head* pounded up and down on the rock. The stern post was carried away and "planks & pieces of wood came to the surface." All hands manned the pumps, trying desperately to keep ahead of the inflow of water that was rising in the hull at two and a half feet per hour. On September 24, with the ship still aground, the crew begged to be allowed to abandon ship. The captain refused the request, pointing out the futility of leaving the ship for the uninhabitable rock, which was still being blasted by bad weather. That day the wind changed again, swinging the gale around to strike from the northeast.

Battered by the wind from a new direction, *Lady Head* bounced over the shoal, dragging anchors and chain behind her. The men on the pumps could not keep pace with the water. Soon it was five feet deep in the hold. By early on September 25, the water was up to the beams, and bales of fur floated free. Knowing he could not save her, Captain Ford gave the order to abandon ship at 8:30 a.m. Passengers and crew launched three boats and pulled away from the wreck, heading due south to Moose Factory, a voyage of 90 miles.

The small, open boats became separated in the storm. The one carrying Captain Ford arrived at Moose Factory at 6:30 p.m. on September 28. The first mate's boat arrived a day later. With their arrival, all the passengers were safe, but the second mate's boat was still out there somewhere on James Bay with five men aboard. To Captain Ford's relief, they rowed up to the post on September 30.

Lady Head had been in trouble in Hudson Bay before. In 1875, under the command of Captain Henry Bishop, she arrived at Moose Factory from London on September 20 and sailed again for England on October 13. En route north for Hudson Strait, she suffered an unspecified accident, almost certainly an encounter with drifting ice, but was able to continue her voyage. On that occasion, she reached London 29 days out from Moose Factory.

Stork was a Swedish-built barque that came to a wintry end on a submerged reef near Charlton Island in James Bay in 1908.
HBC ARCHIVES/ARCHIVES OF MANITOBA 1987/363-S-57/2

Homeward bound for England from Charlton Island in October 1908, the Swedish-built wooden barque *Stork* ran into ice and was forced to return to Charlton. On the way back, she was hit by a blizzard and struck a submerged reef in the whiteout conditions. She was only 22 miles from Charlton Island when she sank. Captain Freakley and his crew escaped in one of the lifeboats and reached Moose Factory just ahead of the winter freeze-up.

Charlton Island claimed a victim in 1910. The HBC had chartered the large Danish barque *Sorine* to act as a supply ship between London and the company's posts in James Bay. Returning in ballast, she suffered damage in the early-winter ice and had to turn back to Charlton Island. She was in such sad shape that her captain, Hans Anderson, deliberately ran her aground on the eastern extremity of Charlton Island. It is probable that the captain and crew hoped to repair her over the winter and kedge her off with ice breakup, but that did not happen. *Sorine* remained onshore and slowly became a hulk.

The HBC's small wooden ketch *Fort Churchill* was a tribute to her Cornish builders. She was not only seaworthy but also capable of sailing long distances without a crew. *Fort Churchill* came down the ways at Porthleven, Cornwall, in the spring of 1913. She was registered in nearby Falmouth and readied for a North Atlantic voyage. The 83-ton ketch, a little less than 74 feet in length, sailed to Hudson Bay and arrived in the Hayes River off York Factory in the fall of that year. After unloading, the crew moved *Fort Churchill* a short distance to the nearby Nelson River, probably to be sheltered for the winter. While at her moorings, and with the captain and crew onshore, a storm blew in and set her free. With no one to guide her, she was at the mercy of the winds and currents that, fortunately, carried her seawards. When the storm passed, the Nelson River mooring was empty. No trace of the ketch was found, in the river or along the adjacent coast. The consensus was that she had foundered, and any cargo aboard had been lost. But the sturdy ketch was very much afloat.

Fort Churchill had gone on a voyage of her own. Keeping clear of the barren southwest coast of Hudson Bay, she travelled at the whim of the winds. Two years after she disappeared from the Nelson River, local Inuit found her aground but more or less undamaged on the Belcher Islands. In April, when the ice began to break up, HBC personnel went to look at the stranded ship and found *Fort Churchill* in remarkably good condition. They were able to refloat her and took her to Moose Factory, where the local shipwright made repairs. She then served as a supply ship in Hudson and James bays for much of the next 24 years. She was finally laid up at Moose Factory in 1939 and burned beyond repair in 1941.

Hudson Bay's notorious weather did not directly wreck the wooden motor schooner *Fort York*; however, it was the major factor that caused her loss. *Fort York* was also built in Porthleven, Cornwall, but one year later than *Fort Churchill*, in 1914. She served her owners well for 16 years—a long time to endure ice, storms and rugged shores—servicing HBC posts on the west side of Hudson Bay. In September 1930, *Fort York*'s luck ran out. Hurricane-force winds attacked the schooner, creating deep concerns for the lives of those on board and the cargo. Her captain, R.H. Taylor, deliberately ran her aground near Fort Severn in order to "protect life and property."

In 1920, the composite-screw sloop *Pelican* was on her final voyage for the HBC when she damaged her propeller in the ice of Hudson Strait. She was fortunate to be near the southern Baffin Island settlement of Lake Harbour, and she managed to put in there for repairs to enable her to reach St. John's, Newfoundland.

The scow *Pagwa*, while not a victim of Hudson Bay, was a regular visitor to Fort Albany on James Bay. She was part of a fleet that transported furs down the Albany River from far inland. In June 1924, *Pagwa* caught fire at the small trading post of English River and burned to the waterline, her remnants sinking later in midstream.

The 100-ton Dutch-built motor ketch *Neophyte* was en route from Baker Lake to Churchill in 1946 when she became frozen in at Chesterfield Inlet. Unable to break the ship free, the crew left her in the ice and travelled to safety by dogsled. *Neophyte* suffered no serious damage and was back in business in 1947, only to run aground and be wrecked on the Severn River bar.

4

Steam on Big Rivers

FROM 1860 UNTIL THE 1940S, the HBC employed close to a score of sternwheelers on a handful of Canada's greatest rivers. They rushed downstream with the fast-flowing current on the mighty Mackenzie, from Great Slave Lake to the vast delta on the edge of the Arctic Ocean, and they fought their way back up again. They saw service on other big rivers such as the North Saskatchewan, South Saskatchewan, Athabasca, Slave, Peace, Liard, Fraser, Thompson, Skeena, Stikine and many more.

The company's first steam-driven riverboat was the sternwheeler *Anson Northup*, built and originally owned by the American entrepreneur Anson Northup. In a dramatic appearance worthy of a theatrical production, *Anson Northup* steamed up the Red River to its confluence with the Assiniboine at Fort Garry on June 10, 1859. The noisy American ship and her brash owner were there as a cheeky challenge to the accepted superiority of the HBC. The intruder from Minnesota looked like a poor reproduction of a log cabin seated on a river scow, her single tall stack belching black smoke and a stern paddlewheel crashing along behind. The ugly apparition was 90 feet long and 22 feet across her beam. She frightened some Fort Garry onlookers and fascinated others.

The company's directors were not amused at the arrival of Northup's creation or the economic threat it posed to them. But they did see the obvious potential of steam-powered riverboats to move freight. As a result, they soon purchased *Anson Northup* through the J.C. Burbank Company for a reported $8,000 and took over the stern-wheeler. She was then refurbished and renamed SS *Pioneer*.

Like a few seagoing HBC ships that would follow, *Pioneer* was crushed by ice—not in the Arctic or subarctic but at Cook's Creek, near Selkirk, Manitoba, in the spring of 1862. Although she was gone, she had served a useful purpose. She had greatly expanded the company's opportunities for trade transportation on the great prairie rivers.

Pioneer's boiler was salvaged and reused in the con-struction of the HBC sternwheeler *Chief Commissioner* in the 1870s. Unfortunately for the company, *Chief Commissioner* was a disaster. Her draft proved too deep for her to work on

Anson Northup (later *Pioneer*) was the first steamboat on the Red River. Her unexpected arrival off Fort Garry on June 10, 1859, created a circus-like atmosphere for onlookers.

A. ROCHESTER FELLOW ENGRAVING, HBC ARCHIVES/ARCHIVES OF MANITOBA P-453

the North Saskatchewan, so she was rescheduled to carry freight and passengers between ports on Lake Winnipeg. Without a keel and almost flat-bottomed, *Chief Commissioner* wallowed dangerously in any conditions other than a flat calm.

After wasting money on the unsuccessful *Chief Commissioner* and losing another riverboat on its maiden voyage, the HBC turned to Scotland for its next nautical adventure. *Lily* was built in sections on the Clyde and shipped to Manitoba, travelling the final stage of her long voyage on the HBC's *Colvile*. She was assembled at Grand Rapids, in the northwest corner of Lake Winnipeg, and put into service. Once again, though, there was a problem. Like *Chief Commissioner*, *Lily*'s draft was a few inches too great for useful service on the North Saskatchewan. The HBC tried various modifications, but none were really success-ful. *Lily* sank on the North Saskatchewan River between Fort Edmonton and Battleford in 1879, after colliding with a submerged rock in broad daylight. The collision tore a big hole in the hull and flooded the ship. She was carrying David Laird, the Lieutenant Governor of the North-West Territories, and a couple of other dignitaries when she set-tled in eight feet of river water. The Lieutenant Governor and his companions remained on board overnight before continuing their journey to the nearest HBC post by row-boat the next day.

Mount Royal was built for service on the Skeena and Stikine rivers of British Columbia and along the coast between the two rivers. She was constructed of western spruce and cedar and measured 130 feet in length with a beam of 28 feet. Powered by two engines, she was designed for hard river conditions, including navigating wild rapids. Her launch on April 9, 1902, was not an auspicious occa-sion. *Mount Royal* got stuck going down the ways, and it took shipyard workers two hours to free her. She then pro-ceeded to stick again. In maritime folklore, a bad or difficult launch day has always been considered a harbinger of bad luck. *Mount Royal*'s career would prove the truth of that superstition.

In May 1906, one of *Mount Royal*'s engines quit running when she was about 20 miles from Hazelton on the Skeena. The passengers had to be ferried to the town by canoe. With the one serviceable engine, the captain and crew managed to manoeuvre the crippled vessel all the way down to Port Essington near the mouth of the Skeena River.

The Skeena is the second-largest river in British Columbia, running 354 miles from the Spatsizi Plateau, high in the Coast Mountains, to the Pacific at Prince Rupert. Renowned for its wildness, the river is too fast and furious for navigation in its upper reaches, and even lower down it can be dangerous. For riverboat captains of the early years of the 20th century, the currents and rapids made every voyage on the Skeena an event. The Stikine is another powerful river with a fierce reputation. Due to a narrow canyon with an extraordinary torrent halfway down its length, it is only navigable from the sea to just above Telegraph Creek.

In July 1907, *Mount Royal* was working through Kitselas Canyon on the Skeena River when a cross-current forced her sideways into Ringbolt Island near Shaman's Whirlpool. Out of control, *Mount Royal* was rolled over by the currents and went under. All the passengers and some of the cargo of furs were saved, but six members of the crew drowned.

The HBC sternwheeler *Mount Royal* loaded with passengers. She was wrecked in Kitselas Canyon on the Skeena River in British Columbia in 1907. WIKIMEDIA COMMONS

Details on the sternwheeler *Saskatchewan* are limited to a few words in the HBC Archives in Winnipeg. She was built expressly for service on the North Saskatchewan River, presumably running between Prince Albert, Cumberland House and The Pas to Mossy Portage at the south end of Cedar Lake, as would another steamer of the same name in the early 1900s. We do know that *Saskatchewan* was wrecked in August 1873, but her engine was saved and used as the power plant in *Northcote*, the next HBC ship built for that river. *Northcote* was launched at Grand Rapids in August of the following year. She worked on the North Saskatchewan River for the HBC for eight years before being sold.

The sternwheeler *D.A. Thomas* was employed, somewhat unsuccessfully, on the Peace River by her original owners, the Lampson Hubbard Company. When the HBC purchased her in 1924, they kept her on the Peace for a few years, but after she grounded hard on a sandbar near Fort St. John in 1929, they accepted that her draft was too deep for that river, and perhaps more important to the HBC, she was not economical to operate because there was not enough freight. The river took care of her through the winter until a spring freshet lifted her off in 1930.

The company directors then decided to transfer *D.A. Thomas* to the Athabasca and Slave rivers. Getting the 175-foot-long and 40-foot-wide ship from the Peace to the Slave without leaving the river meant running her down the notorious Vermilion Chutes. No ship anywhere near the size of *D.A. Thomas* had ever made that run.

The Peace is a wide river, but only a narrow portion of that width is navigable at Vermilion. The chutes extend a mile downstream with an overall drop of only 30 feet. However, above the chutes is a series of rapids with large boulders. At the other end, the river falls over a ledge and builds a large standing wave.

The route *D.A. Thomas* had to follow was narrow—not much wider than her beam. She worked through and down the upper rapids, found her entry to the chute and made good, if erratic, progress to the final ledge. As she tipped over the last hurdle, her bow punched into the standing wave, which broke over her deck, and as her bow climbed the wave her stern paddlewheel hit bottom and was badly damaged. But *D.A. Thomas* had been well built. She completed her run and was then able to continue downriver to Fort Fitzgerald on the Slave River a few hundred miles away. There, for some reason, she was run close to shore and effectively abandoned until she was dismantled later that year.

The sternwheeler *Liard River* operated on the lower reaches of the Liard River between Fort Liard and Fort Simpson on the Mackenzie River in 1918 and 1919. She also is said to have worked on Great Slave Lake. In 1922, she was wrecked on the Fort Nelson River, 35 miles downstream from Fort Nelson.

The log of a smaller HBC boat of the same name describes the problems of navigating the Liard River. The sternwheeler *Liard River* left Fort Simpson on the Mackenzie River at 4:20 a.m. on an August day in 1923. She arrived at the foot of the first rapids on the route about midday. The vessel's log recorded: "Tied up at the foot of the rapids at 12:15 p.m. as the wind was blowing too hard to go through. Pulled out again at 6:30 p.m. and we tried the rapids across the whole of the river. We could not make it so we tied up for the night at 8:30 p.m. The wind was blowing hard all night."

The risks of running the rapids, upstream or downstream, were real. One small incorrect turn of the helm could spell disaster, even for large riverboats such as *Liard River*. On the occasion described above, the wind continued to blow hard in the morning, keeping the vessel tied up until 7:15 a.m. The departure and ascent were far from easy. The log continues: "We had to run a line twice to get over difficult spots in the rapids. We got through the rapids at 2 p.m."

The following day at Flet Rapids, *Liard River* was held up by thick fog, so started late. When she did power up the rapids, it took 75 minutes from the bottom to the top. On an earlier voyage in July, *Liard River*'s crew had stopped at the wreck of her larger namesake and spent four hours collecting anything of value from the remains.

Steamboats ceased to operate on prairie rivers in the late 1890s. They continued on major rivers in British Columbia until the early 20th century and served on the Slave River and the mighty Mackenzie River until the 1950s.

5

Danger on the West Coast

THE COLUMBIA RIVER BAR IS, without doubt, one of the most dangerous entrances to a harbour river in North America, and it is considered by many to be one of the most dangerous in the world. According to the Columbia River Bar Pilots, "The first recorded crossing of the Columbia River Bar by a non-native was by Captain Robert Gray on May 11, 1792. As was the practice of that era, Gray sent the ship's small boat ahead of his vessel to search for the deepest water for safe passage across the shifting shoals and sandbars."

The Columbia River Bar Pilots organization dates back to 1846; the first pilot was Captain George Flavel. It was not before time. According to Oregon State Parks' information, as many as 2,000 ships—and perhaps more—have been lost since the late 18th century while inbound or outbound over the daunting barrier of standing waves between the Pacific Ocean and the Columbia River.

Despite the dangers of the notorious horseshoe-shaped sandbar stretching out into the Pacific Ocean, the 19th-century trading forts on the Columbia River had to be serviced from the sea. Astoria, once an American fort owned by John Jacob Astor, became Fort George in 1813, when the North West Company took over. In 1821, that enterprise merged with the HBC, and Fort George continued in use until 1825, when Fort Vancouver, some distance up the Columbia River, became the main fur-trading fort on the Pacific coast.

William and Ann was a 161-ton brig built in Bermuda in 1818. The HBC purchased her in 1824 and sent her on the long haul to the west coast of North America to set up trading posts and purchase furs to carry back to England. She made at least two successful round-trip voyages from British ports to the Columbia River forts and more-northerly posts.

William and Ann had crossed the Columbia River bar safely a few times from 1825 to 1829. When she arrived in sight of the waves breaking over the bar on March 10, 1829, her captain and crew would have been apprehensive, but not unduly alarmed. However, they certainly should have been concerned, for *William and Ann* did not get across into the calmer waters of the river safely. There is no record of how or why it happened, but the inescapable fact is that *William and Ann* was wrecked on the bar. Little of the hard-earned cargo drifted ashore to reach port. And, although they were all experienced seamen, none of the officers and crew lived to see the end of that day.

The HBC sent another brig, the 195-ton *Isabella*, from England to replace *William and Ann*. *Isabella* safely navigated the North and South Atlantic, rounded the tip of South America and set course first for the Sandwich Islands (Hawaii) and then on to the Columbia River. By the time she arrived off the Oregon coast on May 3, 1830, and aimed her bowsprit in the direction of the Columbia River, she had been at sea more than 180 days. Captain William Ryan then apparently made an error with his bearings and, in a repeat of the *William and Ann* episode, ran the ship up onto a sandbar. All on board escaped with their lives, but the ship became totally wrecked as the waves pounded her for the next week. Much of the cargo was lost.

The brigantine *Mary Dare*, built in an English Channel shipyard at Bridport, Dorset, in 1842, was purchased by the HBC in August 1846. She left England in early November 1846 and spent the next six and a half months sailing to Fort Victoria round the southern tip of South America. Once unloaded, she passed the years from 1847 to 1853 shuttling between the HBC's forts at Vancouver, on the Columbia River; Victoria, on Vancouver Island; and

Honolulu. The 148-ton wooden sailing ship almost met her end at the mouth of the Columbia River in April 1848. Captain James Scarborough was attempting to take her across the bar when the wind suddenly dropped to almost a whisper. The helpless *Mary Dare* drifted into shallower water and grounded on a sandbar. For four hours, she bumped and ground her keel and the bottom of her hull on the sand without suffering more than superficial damage. Captain Scarborough was lucky.

The Columbia River bar was not the only hazard to shipping on the west coast. The HBC also lost ships in California, Washington and as far north as the Queen Charlotte Islands (now Haida Gwaii). The complete coastline, from southern California to the northern extremity of the Inside Passage and Alaska, has a well-deserved reputation for luring ships to disaster.

Two HBC ships named *Vancouver*—*Vancouver I* and *Vancouver III*—were wrecked far to the north of the Columbia River. Both left their remains in the Queen Charlotte Islands. *Vancouver I* was built at Fort Vancouver with substandard materials—unseasoned wood that warped. Despite that drawback, the 100-ton schooner made a number of voyages up the coast for four years, beginning in 1830. On March 3, 1834, under the command of Captain Alexander Duncan, she ran onshore at Point Rose. The wrecked ship and her cargo were left to the Natives when the crew fled in fear.

The HBC schooner *Vancouver I* passes Cape Disappointment to enter the Columbia River.

HENRY JAMES WARE LITHOGRAPH, HBC ARCHIVES/ARCHIVES OF MANITOBA N-5275

Even though he had lost one ship, Alexander Duncan was still given command of the much larger *Vancouver II*, a 400-ton barque built in England. Captain Duncan and *Vancouver II* looked after each other on long voyages from London to the Sandwich Islands and north along what would become known colloquially as the Alaska panhandle. On a return voyage in November 1843, Duncan handed over command to William Brotchie in the Sandwich Islands, probably in Honolulu. Brotchie, in turn, passed the ship over to Captain Andrew Mott in London in 1844, and Mott served her for three years. There is no record of who commanded *Vancouver II* on her fourth voyage to the west coast. Whoever he was, he lost her on the Columbia River bar in May 1848.

Vancouver III was a 192-ton brigantine that had a short life on the west coast. She arrived in December 1852 with Captain James Murray Reid in command. Eight months later, she too went ashore and was wrecked at Point Rose in the Queen Charlottes with another valuable cargo in her hold.

Only 19 months before *Vancouver III* hit the northern islands, the HBC lost the 135-ton brigantine *Una*. Captain William Mitchell had a difficult Christmas in 1851. He was trying to get his ship from the Queen Charlottes to Fort Victoria. In her hold was a small fortune in furs and gold. As *Una* beat her way south off the west coast of Vancouver Island, the notorious winter weather of the region that would later become known as "The Graveyard of the Pacific" threw a gale around her, pounding her into submission. On the night of December 25, the malevolent winds forced *Una* ashore at Neah Bay, near Cape Flattery. The officers and crew, plus the valuable cargo, were saved by the American sloop *Susan Sturgis*. *Una* did not fare so well. Local Natives set fire to the wreck and burned it to a ruin.

The large sternwheel paddle-steamer *Labouchere*, another British-built ship, left London early in September 1858. In the spring of 1859, she arrived on the west coast of North America, where she was to be based. *Labouchere* was over 200 feet in length and sturdily built of Baltic oak and teak. She traded along the Vancouver Island coast until she was refitted in 1866 and transferred to carry mail between Victoria and San Francisco. On her first voyage on the new job, *Labouchere* became a victim of San Francisco's fogs when she ran up on a reef at Point Reyes. She was able to get off by reversing her engine, but she was badly holed and soon flooded until she sank.

The schooner-rigged auxiliary-screw steamer *Otter* almost met a similar fate much farther north. Built in the London shipyard of Richard & Henry Green for the HBC, she sailed from Gravesend for the west coast early in 1853 to become the first screw-propelled ship employed by the company on the Pacific. *Otter* served as a supply ship shuttling between Victoria, a host of small northern ports and San Francisco. During the Fraser River gold-rush excitement, she was seconded to the Victoria to Fort Langley route. She returned to the northern service in 1862 and worked the coast for the next 18 years. On August 21, 1880, *Otter*'s years of safe service were dramatically interrupted when she ran up on a rock near Bella Bella and was holed so badly that she sank. Unlike *Labouchere*, *Otter* was raised, repaired and went back into service for another three years until being sold.

The 131-foot barque *Lady Lampson* made annual round-trip voyages between London and Vancouver Island from 1869 to 1878 without major incident. Each of those journeys spanned the full length of the North and South Atlantic and the South and North Pacific oceans. They also passed through the turbulent waters at the tip of South America. As if to prove the point that most accidents happen close to home, *Lady Lampson* became stranded on Coburg Peninsula on arrival at Esquimalt Harbour on January 10, 1878. She was taken off and sold at auction soon after. Under Hawaiian owners, *Lady Lampson* is said to have been wrecked on Kingman Reef to the northwest of remote Palmyra Island in the Pacific Ocean in August 1893.

From 1824 to 1883, the HBC either owned or chartered close to a score of ships to serve settlements in the Pacific Northwest. The most famous of these ships was the 187-ton paddle-steamer *Beaver*. Equipped with sails as well as two 35-horsepower side-lever steam engines, *Beaver* proved to be an excellent sea boat. She sailed from Gravesend, England, on August 29, 1835, and arrived at Fort Vancouver on the Columbia River 225 days later. The tough little ship served the company well for the next 20 years, working the coast between the Columbia River and ports far up the Inside Passage. Unlike most of the company's vessels on the west coast, *Beaver* never had a serious accident while in the service of the HBC. She was sold in 1874 and thereafter worked primarily as a towboat until she was wrecked on Prospect Point, off the Burrard Inlet, in July 1888. *Beaver* was the first steamship on the west coast of North America and, without doubt, the most famous.

CHAPTER

6

Victims of Arctic Ice

THE JOB OF SERVICING REMOTE ARCTIC trading posts and
missions in the 1920s and 1930s wasn't easy for any ship.
Having achieved a certain success in the eastern Canadian
Arctic, the company's governors in London (none of whom
had been to the Russian or Canadian Arctic) sent a series
of ships into Siberian waters and the western and central
Arctic by way of the North Pacific and the Bering Strait.
The great expeditions that had searched for the Northwest
Passage in the 17th, 18th and 19th centuries had well doc-
umented the difficulties encountered in these waters, but
the HBC ignored much of this evidence. Each one of the
HBC vessels ran into trouble at some point, and many
were fortunate to get out and sail south in safety. Others,

however, succumbed to the pressures of constantly moving ice and left their remains on the seabed.

Of the larger ships, and most of those were less than 2,500 tons, *Baychimo* and *Nascopie* were the best known. They fought the ice every summer for many years and, most of the time, got away with little more damage than buckled plates or broken propeller blades and fractured rudders. Though they both eventually left their scarred and battered hulls deep under the sea in the Arctic or subarctic, they served the HBC well until their respective demises. Other ships were not so fortunate and found the Arctic too powerful an adversary very early in their careers.

The auxiliary-motor–screw Arctic schooner *Lady Kindersley* was built in 1920 expressly for the HBC's service between Vancouver and the company's posts in the western Arctic. Constructed of wood by B.C. Marine Engineers & Shipbuilders Ltd., of Vancouver, BC, she was 187 feet in length with a beam of 36.35 feet. The big schooner was registered at a fraction over 700 gross tons, and her sails were assisted by a two-cycle semi-diesel engine with a four-cylinder power plant from the experienced Scottish engineering company of William Beardmore & Sons of Coatbridge. In consideration of the ice conditions she would be expected to face, *Lady Kindersley*'s hull was almost two feet thick, and her bow was further sheathed with steel. She was, in effect, built as a rather elegant floating battering ram.

Lady Kindersley was designed for service in the Arctic and met her fate there. VANCOUVER MARITIME MUSEUM

After relatively uneventful northern voyages from 1921 to 1923, *Lady Kindersley* motored out of Vancouver's harbour on June 27, 1924, for a voyage around the west and north coasts of Arctic Alaska to Herschel Island and far beyond to Cambridge Bay, on the south side of Victoria Island in the central Arctic. Captain Gus Foellmer, an Arctic veteran, was on the bridge and in command, as he had been for each of her previous voyages. Captain F. Walker was beside him. Walker would be the ice pilot once they crossed the Arctic Circle.

After a difficult voyage from Vancouver, *Lady Kindersley* worked her way into the ice south of Point Barrow, Alaska, 11 days later than planned. En route, she had lost some deck cargo to a typically rambunctious storm in the Bering Sea, and she had suffered engine problems. Now Arctic weather conditions delayed her progress even more, and the engine continued to be a trial. To add to the danger, polar ice closed in around the ship, damaging her rudder and making her impossible to steer. The engineers worked overtime to make repairs, but although none on board knew it, it was already too late. *Lady Kindersley* was trapped and would only be released from the ice's deadly grip once she was crushed to matchwood.

Off the barren coast of north Alaska, Captain Foellmer anchored *Lady Kindersley* to the rafted ice surrounding her and waited. He was nervous. His officers and crew were nervous. The pressure of the ice was unrelenting. A sudden shift in the wind could bring thousands of tons of ice crashing around and over the ship. At breakfast time on August 7, *Lady Kindersley* was about 16 miles northeast of Point Barrow. One worrying week later, the schooner and her icy, open prison had drifted deeper into the ever-moving frozen pack. By this time, she was 56 miles northeast of Point Barrow and still drifting at the mercy of the ice.

Efforts were in progress to rescue the personnel and the cargo—and the ship if at all possible—but the rescue ships were themselves becoming trapped in the same polar ice pack or were blocked by impenetrable ice. Standing by to help in any way they could were *Arctic*, *Boxer* and *Teddy Bear*, and en route, hoping to get close enough to rescue the cargo and the crew, was the HBC steamer *Baychimo*.

Heavy ice stopped the two schooners, *Arctic* and *Teddy Bear*, south of Point Barrow. To add to the difficulties, fog swirled in and blanketed the ships, reducing visibility to a minimum. The crew of *Arctic*, under the command of Captain Bertanccini, blasted the ice with dynamite in a noisy but futile attempt to break free so *Arctic* and *Teddy Bear* could get closer to *Lady Kindersley*'s last known position.

Boxer, a US government vessel, was standing by off Point Hope, some distance to the south, in case she was needed. SS *Baychimo* had been dispatched from Vancouver to assist *Lady Kindersley*, but the long voyage up the North Pacific, across the Bering Sea and through the Bering Strait was slow. *Baychimo* could normally steam at a cruising speed of 10 knots, but in the summer of 1924, when she really needed all her speed to help another ship, she was held up by miserable weather. Strong headwinds and high seas had combined to slow the steamer's northerly progress to a crawl.

Arctic fell victim to the ice when she was crushed in its enormous grip on August 10. *Teddy Bear* continued to search close to the coast, but finding no trace of the ice-bound HBC ship, she gave up on August 16, fought her way out of the ice and sailed south for the safety of Nome's harbour. *Boxer* attempted to reach the trapped ship but was held back for a couple of weeks by the huge ice concentration off Wainwright.

No matter how often the wind changed or from which direction it blew, the ice holding *Lady Kindersley* in its grasp refused to let go. The HBC schooner continued to drift with its deadly white captor. By the time *Baychimo* arrived in the area, toward the end of August, Captain Foellmer was preparing to abandon ship. *Lady Kindersley* was too far into the ice and in extreme danger. On August 31, his crew began the nerve-racking trek across the ice toward *Boxer*, which had managed to reach the edge of the main ice pack. *Lady Kindersley* was left to her inevitable fate.

Boxer transferred the shipwrecked crew to *Baychimo* and then left the area to return to her own schedule. The HBC steamer spent a few days patrolling the edge of the pack ice, hoping for a glimpse of *Lady Kindersley*'s mastheads and a chance to yet save her and her cargo. The efforts were in vain. *Baychimo* gave up the search on September 15 and turned south for Vancouver. The ice-strengthened *Lady Kindersley* was never seen again.

Another elegant three-masted auxiliary schooner, *Baymaud*, had an impressive Arctic career. She was built in 1917 in Norway as *Maud* for the famed Norwegian explorer Roald Amundsen. Registered at 385 tons and measuring 106.8 feet long with a beam of 40 feet, *Maud* was massively built for the job she was designed to do: reach the North Pole by drifting there in the polar pack ice. First, though,

Amundsen had to take the ship to the Beaufort Sea between Siberia and Alaska and find an Arctic current to take them into the polar pack.

After an epic two-year struggle in polar ice from 1918 to 1920, *Maud* arrived in Nome, Alaska, to complete a transit of the Northeast Passage—only the second time that feat had been accomplished. That made Amundsen, who had navigated through the Northwest Passage from 1903 to 1906, the first person to complete a circumnavigation of the Arctic. But he still had not reached the North Pole.

Maud only stayed in Nome a short time, then Amundsen sailed her back to the Arctic. Once again he failed to make any significant headway toward the North Pole. After spending a winter in the ice off eastern Siberia's Cape Serdze Kamen, where *Maud* suffered damage to her propeller, Amundsen gave up the fight and turned south for Seattle. *Maud* later made two more attempts at drifting with the polar pack, but both failed, and each time she returned to Seattle in defeat. Amundsen was forced into bankruptcy and lost his ship to creditors.

The HBC purchased *Maud* in Seattle in December 1925 and renamed her *Baymaud*. The company intended to use her to supply Arctic outposts each summer from the west coast of Canada. *Baymaud* sailed out of Vancouver on June 21, 1926, on what would prove to be a one-way journey. Veteran Arctic navigator Gus Foellmer took command for the northern voyage. The ship passed the usually difficult Point Barrow and zigzagged through the ice off Alaska's north shore to make her first call at Herschel Island. From there, she stopped at a variety of tiny outposts in Coronation Gulf before establishing a new post at Fort Harmon on Victoria Island's southwest coast. The ship then spent the winter across Dolphin and Union Strait in the sheltered confines of Bernard Harbour, on the mainland.

As soon as the ice broke up enough for navigation in July 1927, *Baymaud* went back to work. Having set up the new post at Fort Harmon in 1926, the ship cruised through the uncharted islands of Coronation Gulf to the Kent Peninsula, where the crew tore down the HBC post. They then crossed to Cambridge Bay on the south coast of Victoria Island and built a new post. Once anchored in Cambridge Bay, close to shore, the ship moved restlessly at her mooring, as if anxious to move on. It was not to be.

Captain Foellmer found *Baymaud*'s deep draft to be a liability in the difficult navigation of Coronation Gulf. As a consequence of his report, the HBC decided to leave her in Cambridge Bay as a combined floating warehouse and radio station. The once-proud Arctic exploration ship remained there, moored to boulders onshore by thick wire hawsers, until 1930. That summer, she began to leak through the propeller-shaft bushing. With no possibility of hauling her out and no docking facilities, the problem was ignored, and she gradually filled with water until she sank where she was. Her remains are visible still.

The remains of *Baymaud* show just above the surface of Cambridge Bay on Victoria Island in the Canadian Arctic. ©ANTHONY DALTON

Life in the Arctic might have been cold and unpredictable for HBC ships and their crews, but it was never dull. The motor vessel *Fort James* had a typically exciting career with the company. Built and registered in Shelburne, Nova Scotia, in 1923, for Revillon Frères Trading Company, she was named *Jean Revillon* and put into service in Ungava Bay, Hudson Strait and Hudson Bay. When the HBC purchased a controlling interest in Revillon Frères in late 1926, *Jean Revillon* became an HBC ship and was renamed *Fort James*.

She was a small vessel of only 117 tons with a hardwood hull sheathed in greenheart. That made her a tough little ship. She was further strengthened with internal beams reinforced with concrete. She had handled the drift ice of Hudson Strait and the bay for her first owners; the HBC decided she was strong enough for more strenuous duties.

From 1928 to 1930, she was involved in the company's bid to find a navigable route through the Northwest Passage in order to supply their western Arctic outposts from Montreal. *Fort James* motored up the Davis Strait and round the north end of Baffin Island and into Lancaster Sound. She defied the ice of Prince Regent Sound and squeezed through Bellot Strait. Fighting against ice all the way, she reached her farthest west at Gjoa Haven on the southeast corner of King William Island. There she met a smaller but similar ship, MV *Fort McPherson*, which had travelled east from Tuktoyaktuk. Between them, the two sturdy motor vessels had covered the most difficult long section of the Northwest Passage for the company.

Fort McPherson made her first attempt at working in the Arctic in the summer of 1914, the year she was launched from a Vancouver shipyard. She was prevented from reaching her goal, Herschel Island, that year by ice off northwest Alaska. She was successful on a second attempt in 1915, and in company with the chartered *Ruby*, established the HBC's post on Herschel Island. For the next 15 years, she shuttled back and forth across the Arctic on company business. After meeting *Fort James* at Gjoa Haven, she was wrecked on the return voyage when a storm forced her ashore onto rocks at Richardson Island in the Coronation Gulf. Her crew of five all survived.

MV *Fort Ross* departs Tuktoyaktuk on her way to supply other Arctic outposts. HBC ARCHIVES/ARCHIVES OF MANITOBA 1987/363-F-55/45

Fort James was given a rest from the ice for the next few years. She spent the 1931 and 1932 seasons supplying HBC posts on the often foggy Labrador coast. In 1934, she was scheduled for Arctic service again. That spring, she embarked on the long haul via the Panama Canal, Pacific Ocean and Bering Sea to her new base at Tuktoyaktuk. From there she would collect supplies coming down the Mackenzie River and deliver them to the scattered ports of the western and central Arctic.

The ice of the western Arctic was not kind to *Fort James*. Standing at anchor off Tuktoyaktuk during the winter of

1935–36, she suffered considerable damage from incoming floes. She was repaired, but time and the Arctic were against her. On August 5, 1937, while travelling in convoy with the RCMP ketch *St. Roch*, she was caught in the ice of Coronation Gulf and crushed off Chantry Island. The passengers and crew were rescued by the RCMP and watched *Fort James* disappear under the ice soon after midnight.

The next major HBC casualty in the Arctic was the motor-screw cargo ship *Fort Hearne*, another stout vessel out of the Shelburne, Nova Scotia, shipyards. She spent her maiden voyage travelling through the Panama Canal to British Columbia. From Vancouver, she sailed northwest over the Bering Sea to cross the Arctic Circle and round Alaska to Tuktoyaktuk. *Fort Hearne* made annual voyages delivering passengers and goods to settlements in the Canadian Arctic islands for over a decade without serious problems. Her luck ran out on July 18, 1961, when heavy drift ice rammed a hole through her hull in Dolphin and Union Strait. The Canadian Coast Guard's *Charles Camsell* was close enough to effect a rescue and towed *Fort Hearne* to Bernard Harbour, where she was abandoned.

Fort Hearne's sad end was typical of many HBC ships serving the company's Arctic and subarctic outposts. Heavy ice set in motion by capricious winds and variable currents had endangered Arctic shipping since the first explorers ventured across the Atlantic in search of a Northwest Passage and would continue to threaten any ships attempting to navigate the narrow waterways between Canada's Arctic islands.

CHAPTER

7

Bayeskimo:
Pinched in Ungava Bay

ANY SHIP DEPARTING FOR ARCTIC and subarctic waters runs the risk of battling heavy, drifting ice. Hudson's Bay Company ships had been pushing through the floes and freezing pans on the approaches to the Arctic for over 250 years when *Bayeskimo* joined the fleet. By then, the company and its captains and crews had amassed a store of experience and information on the art of ice navigation. None of that knowledge, however, helped the new ship. She found trouble well south of the Arctic Circle.

Bayeskimo was built in 1922 at Ardrossan, Scotland, to HBC requirements. She was registered at 1,391 tons and was 212 feet, 3 inches long. For three summer seasons, she sailed out of Ardrossan for Montreal to load cargo for the fur-trade posts in Labrador, Hudson Strait and Baffin Island. On the first two successful voyages, she was under the command of Captain Enoch Falk, a knowledgeable and well-respected ice pilot. The equally experienced John Lloyd took over as master for the successful 1924 sailing and was on the bridge again when *Bayeskimo* began preparations for her 1925 voyage.

On June 16, 1925, with Captain Lloyd in command, *Bayeskimo* slipped her moorings at Ardrossan and again made way for the west, loaded with cargo from Britain. After a trouble-free Atlantic crossing, she steamed 1,000 miles up the St. Lawrence River to arrive at Montreal on July 3. There, at the bustling inland port on the great river's north shore, the stevedores unloaded her and immediately began the process of loading again, this time for the North, with freight owned by the HBC, the Canadian government, missions and orders from individuals. Four days after her arrival in Montreal, *Bayeskimo* headed back downstream, on course for North Atlantic waters again and the rugged coast of Labrador. Over the next two months, *Bayeskimo* was scheduled to call at Cartwright, Port Burwell, Fort Chimo (up the Koksoak River at the foot of Ungava Bay), Lake Harbour on southern Baffin Island, Wakeham Bay and Wolstenholme on Quebec's Hudson Strait coast, Coral Harbour on Southampton Island, nearby Chesterfield Inlet on the northwest side of Hudson Bay, then across to the east side of the bay to stop at Port Harrison and Richmond Gulf in Quebec. From there, the itinerary listed a second call at Wolstenholme, a crossing of Hudson Strait to Cape Dorset, Amadjuak and another stop at Lake Harbour. Finally, the ship would stop at Port Burwell again to offload the cargo scows and take on any freight for head office. From Port Burwell, *Bayeskimo* was supposed to steam directly across the Atlantic to Ardrossan.

The voyage down the St. Lawrence was routine. The ship then crossed the northern part of the Gulf of St. Lawrence without hindrance until she was slowed somewhat by patches of fog in the Strait of Belle Isle, the narrow channel between Newfoundland and Labrador. It was a standard cruise from there on to Cartwright, the first port of call on the rugged, indented Labrador coast. The ship arrived on July 12, and the crew had the designated cargo onshore by midday on July 13. Some of it would be transhipped onto smaller boats for carriage to Rigolet, North West River and Davis Inlet. The crew spent that afternoon and early evening taking on new cargo for northern ports and sailed soon after daybreak on July 14. There was a long and difficult voyage ahead, and no skipper of an HBC ship tarried in port longer than absolutely necessary.

Loose patches of ice littered the Labrador Sea, but they were not thick enough to endanger the ship. Captain Lloyd was able to work *Bayeskimo* through the floes and past occasional bergs without difficulty. About 30 miles southeast of Cape Chidley, they met field ice. Despite the ice concentration, tides and currents opened leads and the ship was able to maintain headway to a point northwest of the Button Islands without too much difficulty. There, at the entrance to Hudson Strait and still more than 5 degrees south of the Arctic Circle, Lloyd was faced with ice to the north, west and south. *Bayeskimo* was scheduled to land cargo at Port Burwell. To achieve that anchorage, she needed to find an open route south, down the west side of the Button Islands.

Port Burwell is on the west side of Killiniq Island, just south of Gray Strait. To the west is the huge expanse of Ungava Bay, 140 miles wide where it joins Hudson Strait's south side. The currents in the bay move in a counter-clockwise motion, sweeping ice into the west side of the bay and out of the east where it collides with ice from Hudson Strait and Davis Strait. It was there, where Hudson Strait narrows to 50 miles between the Button Islands and Resolution Island, that *Bayeskimo* was caught.

The ice moved in with relentless intent and stopped the ship. Whenever a lead opened in the desired direction, the captain urged the ship a few yards closer to her destination. Nature, however, had other plans. In an official report, HBC employee J. Cantley wrote, "On the 18th July, after having reached a point only a few miles from Port Burwell, the ice closed in with the tide and carried the ship to the north of the Button Islands again."

Writing his log, Captain Lloyd noted that, "During the afternoon and evening [of July 18] on several occasions the ice exerted tremendous pressure against the vessel's hull."

At first there was no real concern on the captain's part. He had been in similar situations in previous years. As the day wore on and evening descended, however, the earlier air of confidence on the bridge began to give way to concern. J. Cantley wrote, "Previous to that time, while we had been impeded by the ice, the ship had always been kept clear of the bad tidal places where [ice] pressure was to be expected. When caught in the ice and carried back on the 18th however, she was left in a position which was much less favourable and, as the ice remained closely packed, it was impossible to get clear."

That night, heavy ice squeezed the ship's sides and made her groan with pain. Large floes ground against her sides, scarring the black paint. They collected at her stern and worried at her rudder and propeller. The officers and crew could only watch, listen to the torment and wonder how much abuse their ship could take. There was nothing any of them could do; they were quite helpless until the tide changed in the morning and moved the ice away. For Captain Lloyd, with full responsibility for the ship, personnel and cargo, it was a harrowing night. With the morning tide, a wide lead opened to the south, and *Bayeskimo* made all speed for the sanctuary of Port Burwell, only to be stopped by a solid barrier of thick ice about five miles north of the intended mooring.

As if playing with the ship, the ice closed in again on all sides. Crew members checked over the stern and found "the rudder post had been badly twisted and . . . the ship could not be steered." Help was not far away. While the engineering crew worked at full speed to make the necessary repairs and adjustments to the steering chains, another HBC ship, the RMS *Nascopie,* hove into view. She was just in time. *Bayeskimo* was helpless, drifting in the ice's powerful grip toward the Labrador Reef off the Button Islands. If the ice pushed her up on the rocks, she was doomed. *Nascopie* sent over a tow line and made a valiant effort to pull *Bayeskimo* to safety, but the tow line parted, and the work was wasted. Fortunately, *Bayeskimo*'s crew had the steering operational again by this time, and she was able to move under her own steam through patches of slack ice to a safer position northeast of the Button Islands. Once *Bayeskimo*'s steering had been repaired, there was no reason for *Nascopie* to stay. After sending his best wishes to *Bayeskimo,* Captain Thomas Smellie turned *Nascopie* onto her correct course and steamed away. Hoping for a quick run into port in the morning, Captain Lloyd held his ship stationary throughout the night, away from the pressure of the heaviest ice.

On the morning of July 20, a lookout up in *Bayeskimo*'s crowsnest saw a wide stretch of open water about 10 miles off the east coast of Ungava Bay. Captain Lloyd eased his ship south through loose ice formations and found the open water in the afternoon. He was then able to increase speed and reached the latitude of Port Burwell, where the ship laid to for the night about 10 miles out. When the tide changed in the morning, it broke up the ice closer in, and *Bayeskimo* was able to fetch her anchorage on July 21.

The cargo-laden bow of SS *Bayeskimo* forges through the ice of Hudson Strait in 1923. FREDERICK W. BERCHEM, ©MCCORD MUSEUM MP-1984.130.63

While at anchor, Captain Lloyd, his first officer and the senior engineers inspected the hull as best they could, considering the ship was still loaded. The only evidence of damage they found was a single rivet head that had been partly sheared off at No. 3 hold and was causing a slight leak. The chief engineer soon repaired the problem, and as far as they could see, the leak was stopped.

Bayeskimo's next destination was Fort Chimo, up the Koksoak River at the southern extremity of Ungava Bay. The anchor chain clanked up through the hawse pipe, and at 10:00 a.m. on July 22, *Bayeskimo* went back out to battle with the ice. For the first six hours, the going was easy. About 4:00 p.m., lookouts saw the gleam of trouble ahead. Soon afterward, the ship began to work her way through loose field ice, continuing until 10:30 p.m., when hard-packed ice prevented further forward motion. For five hours, Captain Lloyd paced the bridge, keeping close watch on the conditions. He reported, "On July 23 from 3:30 a.m. to 9:00 a.m. the ice slackened and packed repeatedly, but after 9:00 a.m. the ice remained slack and I worked through it at a slow speed."

No one on board noticed any change in the ship's stability at this time, yet there must have been obvious signs of danger. Only two and a half hours later, according to John Lloyd's report, someone noticed a serious problem: "At 11:30 a.m. the vessel appeared to be tipping by the head." In fact, *Bayeskimo* was doing more than just "tipping." She was sinking.

When the engineers took soundings in her holds, they found much to alarm them. There was 10 feet of water in both the port and starboard sections of No. 1 hold. The forepeak held 9 inches of water. No. 2 hold was dry. There is no mention of No. 3 hold in the report, so that is presumed to have been dry as well. Obviously, some important damage forward had been missed by the earlier inspection that found only a damaged rivet beside No. 3 hold.

The engineers started the pumps immediately but could not keep pace with the inflow of water to No. 1 hold. By noon, the water was 16 feet deep in both sides of that hold. Captain Lloyd ordered the crew to jettison the cargo lashed to the foredeck to lighten the load. It was a sensible action but a futile gesture. At 2:30 p.m., it was obvious to all on board that the ship was doomed. Captain Lloyd ordered the lifeboats lowered to sea level and had them filled with food, fuel, drinking water and blankets. He then sent most of his crew and all the passengers from the ship, telling the men in charge of the boats to keep well clear but within "a handy distance."

At 3:00 p.m., No. 1 hold was full and No. 2 hold began making water. *Bayeskimo*'s radio operator sent out a message to his opposite number on *Nascopie*. Captain Smellie radioed back that he was again steaming to their assistance. To keep water away from the fires on *Bayeskimo*, the watertight door to the stokehold was closed. The chief and second engineers, plus a donkeyman, kept the pumps going at full speed, but they could not keep ahead of the rising water. It soon crept into the stokehold. Captain Lloyd reported, "At 8:00 p.m. the [now empty] foredeck was awash, No. 1 hold full of water, and water gaining in No. 2 hold and flooding stokehold. As it was then almost up to the boilers and the stokehold bulkhead appeared to be in danger of collapsing, the vessel was abandoned."

Captain Lloyd, following established maritime tradition, was last off the ship. He marshalled the boats together and had them moored to a large, stable pan of old ice, far enough away to be out of immediate danger. Soon after, watched by her saddened officers and crew from a distance, *Bayeskimo* slid bow first beneath the waves, taking most of her cargo with her. She settled on the seabed of Ungava Bay at approximately 59°15′ N, 67°05′ W. Her wreckage is there to this day.

The crew built two makeshift shelters on the ice, probably from hatch covers, and lit a beacon fire to guide *Nascopie* to them. Captain Lloyd's foresight in having the lifeboats loaded, especially with blankets, probably saved a few lives that night. In the first light of morning, the crew poured gasoline on the fires to make smoke, the better to guide the rescue ship to their precarious position. *Nascopie* arrived at 8:30 a.m. and took all the shipwrecked hands aboard. The following day, July 25, they were landed at Port Burwell and accommodated in the mission buildings. They were also each issued one month's supplies from *Nascopie*'s stores.

Nascopie still had business to attend to in the Arctic and continued north. Once his men were safe on land, Captain John Lloyd left Port Burwell by motorboat with one of his crew and two company personnel: staff members J. Cantley and L.A. Graham and motor mechanic S. Bradbury. Their objective was to follow the coastline and fjords of the east coast of northern Labrador looking for a ship to carry his men south. They called at the Moravian settlements of Ramah, Hebron and Okak before meeting SS *Harmony* at Nain.

John Lloyd asked Captain Jackson of *Harmony* to steam north to collect his crew at Port Burwell and carry them to St. John's, Newfoundland. Jackson agreed to do this, with the proviso that he would have to call at Hebron and Okak en route for stone ballast. Jackson said he anticipated reaching St. John's about the middle of August.

Meanwhile, Captain Lloyd and his companions continued south by motorboat to Ford's Harbour, where they boarded a coastal steamer of the Newfoundland Labrador Mail Service. When their ship called at Makkovik, the first port with a radio station, Cantley sent out a message, in case *Nascopie*'s radio report of the sinking had not been received.

By August 16, they were in Montreal, where Captain Lloyd immediately set to work helping load SS *Peveril*, which was being sent to replace the lost *Bayeskimo* and her cargo. When *Peveril* slipped her lines at Montreal and turned her bow down the St. Lawrence to the open sea, Captain Lloyd was on the bridge with her captain. He sailed north with *Peveril* as her ice pilot.

Bayeskimo had already slid into the depths. Two more company steamships, both with names including the prefix *Bay*, were also destined to leave their imprint on history and their remains on the cold seabeds of the North.

CHAPTER

8

Bayrupert: Lost off the Labrador Coast

THE FOGGY AND DEEPLY INDENTED rocky coast of Labrador has seen its share of shipwrecks. Regularly blasted by ocean storms and seasonally barricaded by drifting ice, it has been a major challenge to navigators since the first boats arrived in Labrador waters.

In October 1885, the HBC's auxiliary barque SS *Labrador* had recently arrived in Rigolet, Labrador, from northern ports to load cargo. The autumn had been unusually stormy, and in early October the winds howled out of the north-north-east, bringing snow and sleet. As their velocity increased, eventually peaking at 125 miles per hour, their power whipped the seas into malignant liquid mountains. The winds and the huge waves were bent on destruction.

Aggravated by the storm, a tidal wave surged across the ocean and slammed into the Labrador coast, creating additional havoc for local shipping.

Labrador was ready to set sail when the massive storm hit the Rigolet area. Captain "Dandy" Dunn kept his crew on watch, his ship at anchor, his sails tightly furled and his boilers with steam up for two anxious days, ready to claw his way to the open sea if the chains parted. All around the ship, the harbour was in chaos. Boats large and small were driven ashore and wrecked, but *Labrador* somehow stayed safe. Beyond, to the east, where the harbour opened to the Labrador Sea, the inlet was said to be "one seething mass of white water." When the storm eased off and the seas began to subside, Captain Dunn's crew hauled in the anchor, and the ship at last made way for the open ocean—and survival.

Forty years later, soon after the loss of *Bayeskimo* in Ungava Bay, the HBC needed a new ship to service the Labrador coast and southern Baffin Island. Furthermore, it had to be ice-strengthened for use in Davis Strait, Hudson Strait and Hudson Bay. The Ardrossan Dry Dock & Shipbuilding Company, of Ardrossan, Scotland, was commissioned to take on the task. The new steamer, to be named *Bayrupert* in honour of the long-dead Prince of the Rhine, was designed to carry a crew of 60 and upwards of 50 passengers, plus she had quarters for up to 64 "Eskimos on the 'tween deck." As she stood ready for launching on March 16, 1926, with only a slide down the greased ways between her and the element for which she was built, she looked hesitant.

Perhaps that hesitancy was an omen, because it took four attempts to launch *Bayrupert*. On the first occasion, she refused all efforts to move her, including the best that power tugboats could provide. Two weeks later, on another high tide, she moved a mere 40 feet toward the sea before she stopped. A third attempt at launching the reluctant ship proved equally unsuccessful. On the fourth try, *Bayrupert* pitched heavily from bow to stern and smacked her keel hard on rocks, damaging the bottom plates. She had to be towed from Ardrossan to Greenock for repairs in a dry dock. Seamen are by nature superstitious. As a result of her reluctance to leave the land and the accident when she did so, *Bayrupert* was considered an unlucky ship.

According to her file at the HBC Archives, *Bayrupert* was 330 feet long with a 50-foot beam. Her draft was listed at 21 feet but would increase to 24 feet or more when loaded. She was registered at 4,037 tons, considerably larger than most of the other HBC ships, and she could steam at 10 knots in open water. A coal burner, she consumed 28 tons every 24 hours. That meant she had to carry 1,680 tons of coal for a typical 60-day voyage.

Captain Thomas Smellie was in command of *Bayrupert* from her launching. He was the HBC's most experienced captain and a veteran of the North. Smellie, born in Hull, England, in 1880, had first gone to sea at the age of nine. After a few years in sail, and after studying and passing examinations for navigation and captain's certificates, he moved on to steamships and eventually became a master mariner. During the First World War, his ship, SS *Crosby*, was absorbed into the HBC and renamed *Baycross*. He subsequently served as master of SS *Bayverdun* until 1917, when he took command of a ship that would become an Arctic legend—RMS *Nascopie*.

On June 3, 1926, SS *Bayrupert* took part in a ceremony at Tilbury Docks, on the north side of the Thames River almost opposite Gravesend, to commemorate the 258th anniversary of the sailing of *Nonsuch*. The historic little *Nonsuch* returned from her epic exploratory voyage to a special welcome in 1669. The modern steamer *Bayrupert* would never see the Thames River estuary again.

In June 1926, Captain Smellie left Tilbury and took his new ship across the Atlantic to Montreal and then north along the Labrador coast, through the Davis Strait and Hudson Strait to Hudson Bay. During the course of that voyage, he took soundings all over Hudson Bay for a new Admiralty navigation chart. *Bayrupert* was his fourth command for the company. He would later take charge of SS *Ungava* before once again being transferred to *Nascopie*.

Two RCMP officers sailed from Montreal on *Bayrupert* for her first voyage into the North. They were destined for Port Burwell to set up and man a police post. Constable Sydney Montague wrote of the ship taking 13 days to reach Port Burwell on a non-stop voyage. When *Bayrupert* steamed away a day or two later, the two policemen watched her go until she was out of sight. Both knew it would be at least a year before she or another company ship came back with more supplies for them. Until then, they were the only two non-Natives in the area. Meanwhile, *Bayrupert* was steaming west in Hudson Strait and on course for Hudson Bay.

At the end of the voyage, Captain Smellie advised the company in writing that, based on his experience, *Bayrupert* was not suited to working the Labrador coast ports due to her deep draft. That coast, he reminded his employers, was littered with islets and rocks and was to a great extent uncharted. A ship the size of *Bayrupert* would be in danger on every Labrador voyage. The powers in London ignored the master mariner's warnings and ordered him to take *Bayrupert* back to the Labrador coast and beyond to Hudson Bay.

There is a saying that reflects the harshness of this rugged coastline: "God made the world in five days, made Labrador on the sixth and spent the seventh throwing stones at it." From south to north, the Labrador coast measures roughly 700 miles. If one considers all the bays and inlets—and there are many—that figure jumps to 4,400 miles. In 1928, a year after *Bayrupert* made her last voyage, the famed and eccentric missionary doctor, Sir Wilfrid Grenfell, commented in an interview that the Labrador coast north of Hamilton Inlet was in desperate need of a survey. Nautical charts of the time, where they existed, were woefully inadequate and inaccurate. It was not surprising that this coast made the master of *Bayrupert* nervous.

SS *Bayrupert* at anchor in Erik Cove in 1926 on her only completed northern voyage. FREDERICK W. BERCHEM, ©MCCORD MUSEUM MP-1984.127.8

The first port of call on *Bayrupert*'s second voyage was Cartwright. The approach to the anchorage was said to be littered with "uncharted shallows." Captain Smellie took his ship in slowly and carefully to drop anchor and no doubt breathed a quiet sigh of relief—one down, many more to go. Ports with equally difficult access followed: Rigolet, Makkovik and Hopedale. The approaches to each one would have added to the strain on the officers. After Hopedale, the next port was scheduled to be Nain, more than halfway up the coast. Sailors are a superstitious breed. Perhaps haunted by a premonition, the captain charted his course to the east to take the ship offshore to deeper water, instead of through the maze of islands that create a scattered barrier along the coast.

Bayrupert: *Lost off the Labrador Coast*

Current. nautical charts show clusters of dots representing natural obstructions extending 15 to 20 miles out to sea. In the 1920s, the Labrador coast still had not been fully surveyed and charted. Without accurate charts, Captain Smellie was, in effect, sailing partially blind. *Bayrupert* passed the Farmyard Islands and continued east for another 15 miles. Satisfied the ship was well clear of any dangers, the captain ordered her head round to the north. The time was close to 7 a.m., and Smellie had been on the bridge for hours, since leaving Hopedale. Now he had a chance to relax for a while. He handed over command of the bridge to his chief officer and retired to his cabin. Weary in his body and with tired eyes, Smellie lay down on his bunk fully clothed and shut his eyes. His body moved with the comforting rhythm of the ship.

On the bridge, the helmsman and the officer in charge swayed with the same rhythm. *Bayrupert*'s bow rose with the swells and settled into the troughs as the ocean moved beneath her. There was nothing ahead except the sea and the sky. Under the surface, however, it was a different story. Uncharted and unknown to shipping, there was extreme yet invisible danger. A pinnacle of rock rose up from the seabed, its apex standing within 22 feet of the surface. No current swirled around it. No waves broke over it to warn of its location. The rock was directly in line with *Bayrupert*'s bow.

Ten minutes after the captain stretched out in his cabin on the morning of July 22, 1927, his ship lifted with another swell. Instead of settling into the next trough as it should have, *Bayrupert*'s bow passed over the unseen rock. As the ship came down, it crunched onto the obstruction and skidded to a halt.

Wide awake immediately, Smellie raced back to the bridge and called for soundings all around and a damage check. There was deep water ahead and astern. Amidships, however, under the boilers, a couple of feet of granite that no one had ever seen or touched had captured the ship. She wasn't holed yet, but the swells would soon take care of that if the ship was not taken off quickly. The crew jettisoned all the deck cargo to reduce weight. The engineers ran the engines full ahead and full astern. *Bayrupert*, impaled on a rock, would not move.

Captain Smellie knew his ship was unlikely to get free and, even if she did, was unlikely to stay afloat for long. The radio operator sent out distress signals, but there were no ships nearby. In fact, the closest ship was 450 miles away. It would take her a day or more to come up. Smellie ordered the 80 passengers and crew into the lifeboats and further loaded them with tents and survival stores. When they were ready, he sent them to make camp on the Farmyard Islands. Only he and the radio operator remained aboard *Bayrupert*, with a single lifeboat tied alongside, in case they had to abandon ship in a hurry.

One passenger, who was in his bunk when the ship struck, had enjoyed his cruise up to that moment. He later commented, "[Sailing on *Bayrupert*] was more like travelling on an Atlantic liner than coming up north."

As night began to fall, the captain and radio operator left the ship and motored over to the islands, where the crew had erected tents and built a huge fire. The accommodations weren't as comfortable as on the ship, but it was a lot safer. By daybreak, the wind had picked up, and the sea was getting rough. Off in the distance, they could see *Bayrupert*. Big waves were breaking over her, making her situation even more desperate. Smellie and a volunteer crew, including the radio operator, returned to the ship to scavenge anything of value and to send out messages about their plight, one of which was to request a salvage ship.

Within two days, SS *Kyle* steamed into sight. She was employed on the Newfoundland-Labrador run. The rescue ship took almost everyone off the island and carried them to St. John's. Only five men stayed behind: Captain Smellie, the chief engineer, radio operator, second officer and the chief steward. They were equipped for a long stay, if necessary. They were soon joined by Natives in whaleboats, who helped strip the ship of everything of value and store it on the island. At this stage, the captain still held out some hope that the salvage vessel would be able to get *Bayrupert* off the rock without incurring additional damage.

The salvage ship's diver put paid to that slim possibility. He went under the ship to find the rock had pierced the bottom of the hull and was poking up through the boiler room. *Bayrupert* was finished.

Five weeks after she hit the rock, her captain and his four companions, plus all the items salvaged from the ship, were picked up by another ship and taken to safety. A subsequent storm lifted *Bayrupert* off the rock and drove her into the deep.

CHAPTER

9

Baychimo:
The Arctic Ghost Ship

ONE OF THE MOST ENIGMATIC stories in the HBC Archives is that of the steamer *Baychimo*. She was built in Sweden in 1914 for a German shipping line for operations in the Baltic. Originally named *Ångermanälven,* the 1,314-ton freighter was handed over to the British government as part of the Treaty of Versailles, which determined First World War reparations. In London, she was sold to the HBC and renamed *Baychimo*. Built with an ice-strengthened bow for the Baltic trade, she was an ideal choice to service the HBC's Arctic and subarctic outposts.

Baychimo first encountered polar ice in Davis Strait while on her initial Arctic mission for the HBC. She was carrying cargo for outposts on both sides of Hudson Strait and on Baffin Island, travelling as far north as Pond Inlet.

Although she ran into heavy ice a few times, she was always able to break free. That was to be her only voyage to the eastern Arctic. The following year she was sent to Siberia.

The intense cold of the Siberian Arctic was a shock to the little steamer and her officers and crew. During her two voyages to the region, she became trapped in ice off the Kamchatka Peninsula, ran aground in a bay near Olyutorka and again in another bay on Siberia's north shore, far above the Arctic Circle. Despite her trials, *Baychimo* not only survived, she acquitted herself well.

Siberia was a tough destination, but the little ship's next assignment, to the western and central Canadian Arctic regions, was even tougher. Although many wooden ships, particularly whalers, had rounded Point Barrow and navigated the ice as far as Herschel Island, no ship of iron or steel had gone that far east along the Beaufort Sea coast.

In 1925, the HBC sent *Baychimo* on a far-reaching Arctic voyage that was to take her from Vancouver all the way to the Bering Sea, then north of the Arctic Circle to distant Herschel Island and way beyond—well over 1,300 miles to the east—to Cambridge Bay on the south side of Victoria Island. The opinion of the cynics on the Vancouver waterfront was that she would never return. In a way, their pessimism was warranted. Accurate charts of the region were non-existent. Her captain, Sydney Cornwell, and ice pilot, Captain Gus Foellmer, would have to rely on local knowledge, their own skills and a huge slice of luck.

The ship had a rough voyage. She grounded a few times. She was pinched in the ice, and she was almost lost to a violent storm at Cambridge Bay, but she came through. Much to the surprise of the old salts in Vancouver, she steamed back in on October 22, battle scarred but triumphant.

During the next seven years of annual voyages to the western and central Arctic, *Baychimo* often limped back to Vancouver or Victoria missing parts of her propeller blades and with significant hull damage from contact with polar ice. But she always came back. The 1926 voyage was perhaps her easiest; *Baychimo* left Vancouver in mid-July and was back on September 20. Year after year, the Arctic ice did its best to sink *Baychimo*, while her master, the ebullient Captain Sydney Cornwell, worked equally hard to get his ship to her northern destinations to deliver hundreds of tons of valuable cargo and to bring her home again in safety.

The 1931 voyage did not begin well. *Baychimo* met the polar ice as she crossed the Arctic Circle on July 25. Most years she had reached Point Barrow a few days after steaming through the Bering Strait. In 1931, it took her until August 21 to cover somewhat less than that distance. Usually, Cornwell had guided his ship to Cambridge Bay by the end of the third week in August and was preparing for the homeward run. Considering the conditions that year, the captain estimated three days to reach Pauline Cove on Herschel Island. It took him closer to four and a half. The season was far advanced, the ice was thick, and the ship still had far to go.

Due to the late arrival at Herschel Island, Cornwell was told to eliminate Cambridge Bay from his itinerary and make his turnaround stop at Coppermine. Even with that revision and the reduced distance, the ship was still expected to call at four small outposts on both the outward and homeward legs. By the time *Baychimo* crashed through the ice to enter Pauline Cove again on her return journey, the calendar read September 12. Herschel Island was completely surrounded by ice. The polar pack was hard up against the north Alaskan coast all the way to Point Barrow and pushing in south of there in the Chukchi Sea for many miles.

Baychimo had never had to winter over in the Arctic, and Captain Cornwell did not relish spending the approaching long, dark months sitting at Herschel Island. He wanted to be at home with his wife in Tunbridge Wells, England, for Christmas. Somehow he had to get the ship past Point Barrow and out of the freezing Arctic seas. But Point Barrow was 400 miles away. In between lay a vast moving field of thick and volatile ice.

The crew hauled anchor at 8:30 a.m. on September 13. By nightfall, the ship was fighting through drifting ice and hindered by snow squalls off the north side of Herschel Island. Returning home from the 1925 voyage, *Baychimo* had taken the entire month of September to get from Herschel to Point Barrow because of the ice concentration. With the conditions so much worse in 1931, Cornwell could not afford to spend so long on the Beaufort Sea traverse. Any delay of that nature would almost certainly cause his ship to be trapped off the Alaskan coast until ice break-up the following summer.

Heading west and making use of every available lead of open water, often no more than a crack wide, *Baychimo* anchored behind rafted ice off Point Barrow on the morning of September 18. There was no open sea in sight. All that could be seen from the crowsnest was ice. The crew waited, impatient to be on the move but with nowhere to go until the wind changed. Three days later, the wind veered round to blow from the northeast, and a narrow lead showed. *Baychimo* followed the opening, her crew hoping to find a navigable route to the open sea. They were disappointed. The wind changed again, and the ice closed in. The ship came to a halt, blocked in all directions. There was another problem: coal for the ship's fires was running low.

By October 8, it was obvious to all on board that *Baychimo* would not be getting out of the Arctic that year. Captain Cornwell moved his passengers and crew ashore and had them build a substantial hut from hatch covers and assorted lumber from the ship. There they would wait until rescue planes could be brought in to fly most of them out. Only the captain and a handful of volunteers would remain behind to watch their ship and, if the opportunity presented itself, get her clear of the ice.

For four weeks, *Baychimo* stood almost motionless, at first only about 100 yards from land, in sight of the make-shift accommodation onshore. As the days wore on, she moved farther and farther away, carried south and west by the restless ice. By the end of October, she had drifted another 400 yards away from land but was still upright.

Pressure ridges built up between the ship and the shore, but she remained visible until a storm blew in late in November. It caused whiteout conditions that kept the men inside their hut for over two days. When the storm died down, the pressure ridges were even higher, with no view of the ship at all. Some of the crew went out onto the ice and risked their lives to climb the massive ridges. From the summit they had expected to see *Baychimo* tucked comfortably against the other side. Their hopes were dashed. *Baychimo* was not there. Her 1,314 tons of steel and wood had vanished.

The obvious initial conclusion was that she had been holed or crushed by the ice and sunk. That had been a real possibility for weeks, so the ship's disappearance was not entirely unexpected. Despite that, Captain Cornwell and his men searched the coast in both directions, hoping to find the ship safe. They searched in vain. Another storm blew in and lasted for many days. When it was over, two Alaskan trappers working south of the hut shook the snow from their eyes and looked out to sea—at a ship. *Baychimo* had survived and returned.

The derelict SS *Baychimo* was photographed by visitors from a trading schooner two years after she was abandoned in the ice off Alaska's northwest coast. HBC ARCHIVES/ARCHIVES OF MANITOBA 1934-2-2

The trappers boarded her and removed some bales of furs. They then went to Cornwell and told him what they had seen and done. The captain went out to look at the ship for himself, but he could do nothing to prevent her from sinking or disappearing again. She was a prisoner of the ice, and it was impossible to set her free. *Baychimo* and her prison were there to tease.

The tough little ship had embarked on a long and convoluted voyage of her own. Over the next three or four decades, *Baychimo* drifted alone and empty for thousands of miles through the Arctic wastes, trapped in a large pan of old ice. She was photographed, boarded a few times and looted of anything of value. She never stayed anywhere for long, becoming a ghost ship that sailed silently wherever the ice, winds and sea currents took her.

No one knows where or when *Baychimo* finally succumbed to the relentless pressures of the ice. No trace of her has been seen for over four decades now, at least, so it is certain that her crushed remains litter the seabed somewhere in the Beaufort or Chukchi sea. Perhaps scientists using modern technology will find her one day and close the last chapter in the remarkable life of a rather extraordinary ship.

10

The Ravages of War

EARLY IN THE FIRST WORLD WAR, the HBC and the French government entered into an agreement whereby the HBC would charter enough ships to transport millions of tons of much-needed supplies from Allied countries to French ports. The HBC set up subsidiary companies, one of which was called The Bay Steamship Company. Those entities chartered 286 cargo ships on behalf of France, totalling over a million tons. In four years of operation, those ships carried 13 million tons of cargo. The HBC, of course, earned a considerable sum of money—said to be well in excess of $5 million—as its share of the net profits from the venture. Of the large fleet assigned to the French operation, most were in the 3,000- to 5,000-ton range, although in 1917, four bigger Russian passenger ships, each around 13,000 tons, were added to the fleet.

These ships and others already owned or employed by the HBC flew British pennants from the flagstaff, which made them automatic targets for marauding German submarines. During the war years of 1914 to 1918, no one knew where these manmade predators of the sea might strike next. They roamed the Atlantic, the Mediterranean, the English Channel, the North Sea and beyond.

SS *Feliciana* was built by Northumberland SB. Co. Ltd. of Newcastle in 1909. On April 21, 1916, *Feliciana* was outbound from London and Cardiff to New York in ballast. Her voyage was cut short when she was identified by the German submarine U-19 and torpedoed 67 miles west of Fastnet Rock, the most southerly point in Ireland. There were no reported casualties.

Six months later, in the same general area, SS *Bayreaulx* took a hit. A few years older than many in the fleet, she was built in 1895. *Bayreaulx* left Cardiff in ballast for Montreal with a crew of 23 aboard. A few days later, on October 23, 1916, she was torpedoed somewhere west of the Scilly Isles and south of Ireland's Cape Clear. There were no survivors.

Launched as SS *Dinsdalehall* at Hebburn-on-Tyne in 1906, SS *Bayhall* was carrying a cargo of sugar from Mauritius to Bordeaux when she encountered a U-boat in the Bay of Biscay about 90 miles north of Cape Ortegal, Portugal, on December 17, 1916. The U-boat commander captured the freighter and crew and sunk the ship with explosives.

The first day of January 1917 was not a good day for SS *Baycraig*. Built by Wm. Pickersgill & Sons of Sunderland in 1905, she was in the Mediterranean Sea inbound from Port Louis, Mauritius, to Marseilles when she was torpedoed 84 miles east-southeast of Malta. She too was carrying sugar and took the full cargo to the seabed with her.

Sugar, indirectly, was the cause of another HBC ship's explosive end. SS *Baynesk*, built by the famed Sunderland yard of William Doxford in 1906, was only hours out of the Mediterranean end of the Suez Canal, en route from Mauritius to France, when she was torpedoed by U-boat UC-39 on January 9, 1917. She went to the bottom with seven casualties.

Occasionally, one of the ships would be destroyed by accident, instead of by enemy fire. SS *Bayropea*, built in 1905 by Armstrong Whitworth, sailed from Cardiff to the Russian port of Archangel in the White Sea with a cargo of munitions. She caught fire at her destination and blew up, fortunately without casualties, on January 26, 1917.

SS *Holgate* joined the HBC's temporary wartime fleet in August 1916. She was sent to Archangel, where she loaded a strangely mixed cargo of wheat and a few cannons for shipment to Nantes on the Bay of Biscay. From the French port, she sailed for Penarth in Wales and possibly was signed off the company's books because there is no record of additional activity for her on HBC business. The following March, she was hit by a German torpedo and sunk.

SS *Baynaen* steamed away from Java loaded with sugar for France early in 1917. She navigated the Indian Ocean, Red Sea, Suez Canal and the Mediterranean in safety. Then, on March 25, she was sunk by a torpedo in the Bay of Biscay, only hours from her destination of Nantes. Built in 1904 at the William Doxford yard, *Baynaen* was 3,227 tons. Five members of the freighter's crew died in the attack.

SS *Tung Shan* passed through the Straits of Gibraltar carrying coal from Tyneside to Genoa. With the Rock of Gibraltar falling astern, she set a new course for the west coast of northern Italy. Like so many ships before her, she didn't reach her destination. On May 15, 1917, she was captured by the German submarine U-34 in the Gulf of Valencia. The submarine's crew scuttled *Tung Shan* seven miles north of Cape San Antonio.

SS *Baysoto*, built in 1905, was sighted on August 6, 1917, by the German submarine UC-42 and sunk by a torpedo just 33 miles southeast by east of Girdleness, on Scotland's northeast coast. *Baysoto* was on a voyage from Archangel to Tyneside and Le Havre with a cargo of flax. There were no reports of casualties.

SS *Baychattan* was an armed, 3,758-ton merchantman. She was built by Charles Connell & Co. of Scotland in 1906. *Baychattan* was on a short voyage across the English

Channel from Le Havre to Cardiff when she was hit by a torpedo on October 11, 1917, close to Prawle Point in Devon. The U-boat had attacked without warning, and the freighter paid the ultimate price.

The 24-year-old SS *Bayvoe* crossed the stormy Atlantic in winter without incident, carrying a full cargo of American wheat. While on the final stretch of her voyage from Portland, Maine, to Bordeaux, France, she was torpedoed on January 9, 1918, by the German submarine U-84 in the Bay of Biscay. Four members of her crew were killed in the assault.

SS *Baygitano* was a product of John Readhead & Sons of South Shields, Northumberland. Built in 1905, she was registered at 3,075 tons. Armed for her own defence for the duration of war, *Baygitano* did not have a chance to fight. Although she was in Lyme Bay, within sight of the southern English coastal town of Lyme Regis, she was torpedoed and sunk by a U-boat on March 18, 1918. Two of *Baygitano*'s crew died as a result of the attack.

Not all the ships that encountered submarines became casualties. The HBC's *Pelican* fought a German submarine in August 1918 and survived. She was a composite-screw sloop launched at Devonport, England, in April 1877 for the British Admiralty. Purchased by the HBC in 1901, she was strengthened for work in the ice of Hudson Bay and adapted to carry cargo. Two years after the war had ended and *Pelican* had returned to normal service, her propeller was badly damaged by ice in Hudson Strait. She put in to Lake Harbour for temporary repairs before making way for St. John's, Newfoundland. *Pelican* was one of the luckier ships.

Another lucky ship, for most of her working life, became something of a legend. While she was working in Russia's White Sea in June 1917, with Captain Edmund Mack in command, the famed RMS *Nascopie* had a tussle with a German submarine and got away due to her audacity. *Nascopie* had steamed out of Archangel bound for Lerwick, Shetland Islands, and onward to St. John's, Newfoundland. On the first day out, while still in the White Sea, a torpedo was seen streaking past the ship's stern. The captain ordered full steam ahead and ran for safety. The following day, as *Nascopie* worked through loose ice, lookouts sighted a submarine. The submarine fired a shot at the freighter, missing it by a couple of hundred yards. Captain Mack had his ship turned stern on to the attacker and fired back, but missed the target. The submarine fired again and also missed. For the next few minutes, as *Nascopie* zigzagged through the ice pursued by the deadly predator, both vessels fired at each other without success. Then, manoeuvring through the ice, the submarine exposed its flank, and *Nascopie*'s gunner took careful aim. Captain Mack reported, "Collins [the gunner] took what seemed an agonizing long time to fire, but when he did the Lord was with him. It was a shot in a million and landed fair and square on the submarine's gun mounting.

Then *Nascopie* stopped. Four more shots from Collins and there was a big explosion. Black smoke and flames shot high in the air and there was no more submarine."

The U-boat is believed to have been U-28. German records show it was in the area and involved in an action against a ship on that day, but they claim it was not damaged and that the smoke and flames seen were produced to camouflage the submarine's escape. *Nascopie* survived that potential tragedy and would survive many more life-threatening situations in Arctic ice, but her eventual end perhaps had already been decided. Was that decision made by fate, or by other forces?

And then there was SS *Baynyassa*. Like most of the HBC vessels torpedoed or scuttled in the First World War, *Baynyassa* was only a temporary member of the company's extensive fleet. She was built by Bartram & Sons of Sunderland, England, in 1915, but we know little else about her other than the basic facts of her demise. The 4,937-ton steam freighter was on a trans-Atlantic voyage from Santos, Brazil, to Gibraltar when she ran aground on the desert coast of Morocco a few miles south of Agadir on September 15, 1918. On that occasion, rather than destruction by enemy action, the ship was almost certainly wrecked by human error. Because they were so close to a level, sandy beach—the western fringe of the Sahara—all on board were able to get ashore and there were no casualties.

SS *Baynyassa* was on a voyage from Santos, Brazil, to Gibraltar when she ran ashore on the Moroccan coast south of Agadir in 1918. WWW.PHOTOSHIP.CO.UK

By the end of the war, The Bay Steamship Company had lost 110 ships—an aggregate dead weight of 475,000 tons—to enemy action, most of those to submarine attacks. Collectively, those vessels were worth £11 million and contained cargoes to an estimated value of £14 million. Despite those losses, the ships and their stalwart crews had kept the French people supplied with food and other much-needed supplies, such as munitions and coal, for four desperate years. At the close of 1919, over a year after the war ended, the HBC still owned and operated just under 100 steamships.

CHAPTER

11

Bayronto and the 1919 Florida Keys Hurricane

IN SEPTEMBER 1919, *BAYRONTO*, a British-built freighter, leaned against the dock in Galveston, Texas, while hundreds of tons of American wheat gushed into her holds. Dust clouds filled the air and covered the ship and her sweaty crew as they worked on deck in high humidity. The local stevedores, accustomed to the extreme heat, suffered with them. As soon as the wheat was loaded, *Bayronto* would prepare for a voyage that would take her across the North Atlantic and into the Mediterranean Sea and the French port of Marseille.

Bayronto was one of many freighters pressed into the combined service of the French government and the HBC during the First World War. Built in 1905 by the Armstrong

Whitworth Company of Newcastle, England, she had survived a torpedo attack by a German submarine in the summer of 1918 and, although damaged, had made port safely. Now, in the first year of peacetime, her voyages should have been routine and relatively safe, but trouble was brewing far to the east and south.

On September 1, 1919, a tropical wave was identified in the vicinity of the Lesser Antilles. It was not an unusual occurrence: about 100 tropical waves form during each hurricane season in the Atlantic and off the eastern Caribbean. One day later, the system was upgraded to a tropical depression as it passed Guadeloupe. It still was not dangerous, but meteorologists watched carefully for signs of increased activity. On September 3, while the fledgling storm moved northeast toward Puerto Rico, it was categorized as a tropical storm. The southwest corner of Puerto Rico was hit by 50-mile-per-hour winds as the storm passed but only sustained minimal damage. Then the storm turned north briefly, arcing between Puerto Rico and the larger island of Hispaniola. Once through the strait between the two land masses, it turned west, running parallel to Hispaniola for the next two days and getting stronger with each passing hour. The storm was over the Bahamas by September 7 and had been upgraded to a Category 1 hurricane.

Long before the advent of radar or weather-spotting aircraft, the only way to track a storm was to rely on reports from ships in the area or from human coastal watchers.

Sometimes storms or hurricanes such as this one would disappear for a day or two as they passed out of range of ships and binoculars. Few, therefore, could accurately predict where such disturbances would travel next or where they might hit land.

At Galveston, SS *Bayronto* was in the final loading stages. Once she left port, her course would take her directly across the Gulf of Mexico to pass between Cuba and the Florida Keys. From there she would steam past the Bahamas and into the Atlantic Ocean. *Bayronto* was not the only ship preparing for departure or already on the Gulf of Mexico. Nine other ships were in the general area. Between them, the vessels carried hundreds of passengers and crew. One of those ships was the Spanish passenger steamer *Valbanera*, en route from Spain to ports in Cuba and on the American gulf coast. She arrived off Havana on September 8, having off-loaded over 700 passengers at Santiago de Cuba a few days earlier. Because of the hurricane-force winds, she was unable to enter harbour and signalled that she would ride out the storm on the open sea. At that time, *Valbanera* was said to be still carrying 400 passengers and 88 officers and crew.

The hurricane, the only one to develop in Atlantic waters that year, would prove to be the second-most deadly hurricane on record up to that time. Estimates of damage would reach $22 million and the number of lives lost would eventually tally in the high hundreds. At its peak, the hurricane powered winds of 150 miles per hour near Key West on

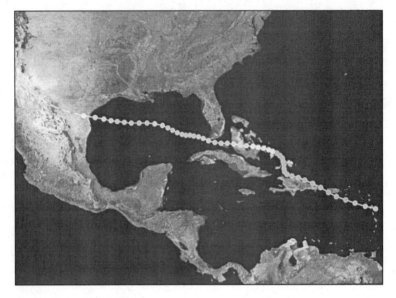

The deadly path of the 1919 Florida Keys hurricane that sank the HBC freighter *Bayronto* in the Gulf of Mexico. WIKIMEDIA COMMONS

September 10. Those extreme winds created havoc on any land over which the hurricane passed. Eight former US Navy patrol boats moored in North Beach Basin at Key West were wrecked by the hurricane as it passed on September 11. The damage at sea was far worse. Waves well in excess of 20 feet coursed across the Gulf of Mexico with the hurricane.

Eleven days after she was seen off Havana, *Valbanera*'s wreckage was spotted by a US Navy sub-chaser near Rebecca Shoal, 45 miles west of Key West. Only her mast and two lifeboats were visible. No trace of the 488 people aboard was ever found.

Bayronto left Galveston with a heavy load of 7,000 tons of wheat, causing her to sit low in the water. Her captain would have known about the approach of a hurricane but would not have known it was in his path. His first clue would have been the rapid increase in the size of the waves, followed by the strength of the wind. The hurricane's incredible power bore down on the 6,400-ton ship with ominous precision. The screaming winds and massive waves smashed into her, tossing her 400-foot length around like a toy. She rolled from side to side and from end to end, the wind shrieking across her deck and blasting the bridge. All crew would have been ordered to stay below. No man could survive on deck for more than a few seconds without being swept away. The waves slammed into her from all sides, sweeping her deck clean and weakening her hull. On September 13, far off course to the north of her planned route and unmanageable in the tempest, *Bayronto* began to break up under the sustained assault. The captain ordered all hands to abandon ship, even though only two lifeboats were serviceable, the others having been wrecked by the pounding. With no hope of salvation, Bayronto broke in half and turned over. She disappeared beneath the sea with her perishable cargo as her crew fought for their own survival above.

Somehow, a fishing smack named *Ida* rode out the storm and found 11 of the crew alive and well. She carried them to Tampa, Florida. At least another six fishing boats were lost as the hurricane gave no quarter. Meanwhile, the SS *Calno* picked up 19 other members of *Bayronto*'s crew and carried them to Charleston, South Carolina. A further 18 lucky survivors were also found and taken to Havana. *Bayronto* had gone to her grave, but much to their surprise, all her officers and crew lived to return home and tell their own tales of the hurricane.

The wreck of *Bayronto* is in two main pieces, upside down on the sandy bottom of the Gulf of Mexico, some 30 miles offshore from Venice, Florida, in 110 feet of clear warm water. Sited at approximately 26°45' N, 82°50' W, today she is a haven for marine creatures of all kinds and a major exploration site for divers from all over the world.

12

Nascopie:
On a Cape Dorset Rock

CAPE DORSET IS ON Mallik Island, off the south shore of the Foxe Peninsula at the western end of Baffin Island's Hudson Strait coast. It was named by Captain Luke Foxe in 1631 while he was exploring the region by ship, looking for a route through the Northwest Passage. The cape is protected from the sea by a row of similarly sized islands with access from the south by way of the West Inlet and from the east by passing Apalooktook Point. The most distinguishing feature of Cape Dorset, and an excellent landmark from the land or the sea, is a big rounded mountain of granite that climbs 798 feet high as a coastal feature of the Kinngait Range.

Long before Foxe arrived, the local Inuit, now known as the Cape Dorset Culture, had lived and hunted in the area from 1000 BC to 1100 AD. A few of their descendants live along that part of the coast to this day. Once hunters, they are now world-renowned artists.

There are seals in abundance in Hudson Strait, and polar bears, while caribou herds and Arctic foxes roam the land. In summer, the interior of the Foxe Peninsula is a breeding ground for many species of migratory geese and ducks. Because of fur-trading opportunities offered by the region, the HBC set up a trading post at Cape Dorset in 1913. With aviation not yet a viable transportation option, the only sure way to receive supplies and move the furs to the outside world was by sea. When the HBC post was established in 1913, all the building materials, plus the post manager, arrived in a new ship.

RMS *Nascopie* was a steel-hulled steamship built specifically for the HBC fleet. A product of Swan, Hunter & Wigham Richardson's Neptune Works at Wallsend-on-Tyne, near Newcastle, England, she was intended for summer service along the Labrador coast and north into the subarctic and Arctic, including calls at Cape Dorset.

Nascopie was 285 feet long with a beam of 43 feet and was registered at 2,520 gross tons. Although she was not built as an icebreaker, she was ice-strengthened and had been designed with an undercut bow and a rounded hull without an external keel. Those features meant she could be forced over ice to break it with her weight without being trapped. She slid down the ways to enter the River Tyne on

December 7, 1911. A crew of skilled Newfoundland sailors waited at Wallsend to take her down the North Sea and west along the English Channel to load up with coal at Penarth in Wales. Loaded and ready for sea duty, *Nascopie* crossed the North Atlantic for the first time in January 1912, under the command of Captain A.C. Smith, and worked for the remaining winter months on sealing voyages out of St. John's, Newfoundland, but with Captain G. Barbour on the bridge. That summer, with Captain Smith again in command, she made the first of her many voyages to the North. Smith was replaced in 1913 by Captain J. Meikle for one voyage but took over again in 1914. Captain E.G. Mack, who had been second officer on the maiden voyage across the Atlantic, took command from 1915 to 1917.

In 1916, *Nascopie* was transferred to the HBC fleet working for the French government as part of its First World War efforts. The Arctic steamer was put into service shuttling supplies between the French channel port of Le Havre and the Russian port of Archangel in the White Sea. On one wartime voyage, *Nascopie* survived a confrontation with a German submarine. Captain Thomas Smellie replaced Mack in 1917. He would become almost as famous as his ship, and his name would forever be synonymous with that of *Nascopie*.

After the war, *Nascopie* carried a herd of reindeer and their Lapp herders from Norway to Baffin Island. She then returned to her peacetime role of supplying northern outposts. A typical trading voyage for RMS *Nascopie* in the

1920s and 1930s would take her from Montreal on a journey of 9,000 miles or more into the Arctic, subarctic and Hudson Bay. On any one voyage she would visit posts as diverse as Cartwright on the Labrador coast; Port Burwell, Lake Harbour, Amadjuak and Cape Dorset on southern Baffin Island; Wolstenholme and Sugluk in northern Quebec; then the Hudson Bay ports of Churchill, Chesterfield Inlet, Coral Harbour and Charlton Island before returning through Hudson Strait to St. John's and Montreal. Often she would go much farther north to Pangnirtung, Pond Inlet, Arctic Bay and Dundas Harbour.

Nascopie's passengers were HBC employees, Mounties, mission people, traders and assorted Arctic residents, and sometimes their families, plus occasional dignitaries and a few famous names. In 1924, Captain Smellie welcomed renowned Danish Arctic explorer Peter Freuchen aboard near Chesterfield Inlet. Freuchen had frostbitten toes that required amputation, and *Nascopie*'s doctor performed the operation on the ship. On the 1926 voyage, naturalist J. Dewey Soper travelled on the ship from Amadjuak to Port Burwell. Soper would go on to become the most important Canadian naturalist and Baffin Island explorer of his time.

There was a change of schedules for the summer of 1927. *Nascopie* sailed out of St. John's to make two round trips to Hudson Bay in one season, but not across the Arctic Circle. As winter took hold on the Maritimes, she was sent on a sealing expedition out of St. John's. She returned to regular northern and Arctic service in the summer of 1928 but continued to work on sealing voyages in the winters of 1928 to 1930. Because of the effects of the worldwide economic depression, *Nascopie* spent the next three years laid up in Scotland, during which time she had a substantial refit and upgrading of equipment before sailing to Montreal with Thomas Smellie on the bridge. Montreal would remain her home port for the rest of her life.

In 1937, the little Arctic ship eclipsed even her own spectacular northern voyages by steaming through almost impossible ice conditions in Prince Regent Inlet to meet MV *Aklavik* at Fort Ross on the east shore of the Boothia Peninsula. *Aklavik* had fought through the ice-constricted Bellot Strait, inbound from the Mackenzie Delta. With that historic meeting, two ships of the HBC had bridged the forbidding Northwest Passage.

During those epic forays into the North each summer, *Nascopie* called many times at most of the accessible settlements on the Labrador coast, each HBC trading post in Hudson Strait, Ungava Bay and the vast reaches of Hudson Bay. In addition, she stopped at all the posts on Baffin Island's coasts and throughout the eastern Arctic.

With the advent of the Second World War, *Nascopie*'s traditional black hull was painted grey to disguise her profile as much as possible. She still steamed to the Arctic most summers but also worked on convoys to the Caribbean and made solo voyages to the west coast of Greenland.

RMS *Nascopie* is framed by ice at Port Burwell in 1937.
HBC ARCHIVES/ARCHIVES OF MANITOBA 1987/363-N-7A

By the time she returned to Arctic service after her busy few years during the Second World War, *Nascopie* was old and tired. Her long-serving master, Captain Thomas Smellie, was tired too. He had looked after the ship from 1917 to 1919, from 1922 to 1925 and again from 1933 to the final day of 1945, when he stepped down from the bridge for the last time.

Thomas Smellie handed over *Nascopie*'s keys to Captain James Waters, who had been chief officer under Smellie since 1941. Captain Waters commanded her 1946 voyage to Hudson Bay and delivered her back to Montreal five days early. On that voyage, for the first time, *Nascopie* had the benefit of radar to help navigate deeply indented coastlines and avoid heavy ice and icebergs.

Nascopie's planned 1947 itinerary was typical of the routes she had followed for over a decade, with only few variations. Sailing from Montreal on July 5 with flags flying and a heavy load distributed throughout her holds and on deck, she was scheduled to call at Cartwright, Labrador, to pick up her barges, which had been left there the previous September. From there, she would continue on to Lake Harbour on the south shore of Baffin Island, across Hudson Strait to ports such as Sugluk and Wolstenholme in northern Quebec, back across the strait to Cape Dorset on Baffin Island's south coast, and onward to Southampton Island and ports in Hudson Bay.

Nascopie's 1947 voyage was different from those of previous years. In many ways, it was a mission of mercy. The passengers were mostly doctors, dentists, nurses and associated medical scientists going north on behalf of the Canadian government to open clinics and administer health care to the indigenous people of Canada's Arctic for the first time.

Though many of the passengers were new to the sea and to the Arctic, *Nascopie* was a worn veteran of 36 hard years. She had spent 31 summers in the Canadian Arctic. She had punched her way through the ice north of Scandinavia and Russia for a further four summers and had survived two world wars. She was tough, but her machinery was getting old, and her hull had taken regular beatings from ice. Also, she was no longer economical, burning far larger quantities of expensive coal per day than more modern steamships.

For months there had been communiqués passing around the HBC head offices in London about a replacement for the aging steamer. *Nascopie*'s hard life working for the HBC was almost over, but without an alternative ship to take on the northern route, she still had to make the 1947 subarctic voyage.

Nascopie was no stranger to the dangers of Hudson Strait or the confined entrance to Cape Dorset. The steamer had been calling in at the remote HBC and RCMP post since her earliest northern voyages for the company. However, on the 1947 voyage, as during the previous year, she had the advantage of radar to assist the navigation. Radar would ease the strain on the lookouts as *Nascopie* moved among the drifting icebergs and approached land, which was often obscured by sea fog, heavy rain or driving snow. Radar was an extra pair of eyes that could see where no human eyes would work efficiently.

According to at least two observations on the weather that day, "the sky was overcast and threatening, but the sea was smooth" as the ship steamed away from Wolstenholme on the morning of July 21. There was little ice in the strait to hinder progress, so *Nascopie* passed the east end of Salisbury Island and turned almost due north for the remote Baffin Island post. She hove in sight of the mountain that marked Cape Dorset as planned in the early afternoon of that day.

Captain Waters chose not to use the services of a Native

pilot for the final approach to his anchorage, even though the experienced Peter Pitseolak was available and offered his services. Instead, Waters relied on his depth sounder, radar and the lookouts. Waters was apparently unaware of an uncharted reef rising almost straight up from the seabed just off Beacon Island at the entrance to Cape Dorset. By the time the depth sounder picked up the obstruction and reported it, *Nascopie* was too close. Waters rang down for engines hard astern, but it was too late. The ship rode up on the rock and stopped. With a rising tide, she floated off when the water reached a certain level. The captain ordered the anchor dropped and the engineers soon had the pumps working hard.

It was not enough. The damage to *Nascopie*'s hull was too extensive. The pumps could not keep up with the water flowing in. Then, to add to the already dangerous situation, the weather began to deteriorate as night fell. Sometime near 3:00 a.m., Captain Waters gave the order to haul anchor. By this time, the ship had taken on a large quantity of water, and she could not be steered properly unless under way. But before she could start moving, the current gained hold and swept her back onto the reef. Waters called down for full astern, but it was too late. The current swung the stern onto other rocks, and that, in effect, was the end of *Nascopie*'s illustrious career. She was hard aground, supported by immovable rock. Because there was no immediate danger of *Nascopie* sliding off the reef, the passengers and crew were able to get off in lifeboats.

Captain James Waters (left) and his officers look across the bay to RMS *Nascopie* trapped on a rock at Cape Dorset, Baffin Island, in 1947. HBC ARCHIVES/ARCHIVES OF MANITOBA 1987/363-N-8D

Nascopie remained stranded on the reef with a large gash in her hull for close to three months. During that time, she was visited and boarded regularly by residents of Cape Dorset. Crew members went back on board and rescued the mail, the ship's bell and some food and clothing. Strangely, considering their importance, none of the officers or crew saw fit to remove the logbooks of that final voyage. Those valuable documents, the factual history of the last voyage of the RMS *Nascopie*, went down with the ship when she scraped herself off the reef and sank into deep water on October 15, 1947.

It was inevitable that questions would be asked about the sinking, both officially and unofficially. The ship was close to the end of her useful working life. Why were the all-important logbooks left on board when they could so easily have been retrieved during the many weeks the dying ship rested on the reef? Was *Nascopie*'s ignominious end deliberate? We will never know.

Epilogue

THE HBC'S SEA-TRANSPORT ERA ended in 1987, when the company sold MV *Kanguk*, its last ship. *Kanguk*, a sleek 1,599-ton freighter, could carry over 3,000 tons of freight and was handled by a crew of 22 men. She was built in Sweden in 1964 and purchased by the HBC in 1982. Like many other company ships, *Kanguk* had her own brushes with disaster but was fortunate to escape. Soon after she joined the HBC, *Kanguk* ran aground in the mouth of the Povungnituk River, in Quebec, on the east side of Hudson Bay, and extensively damaged her hull. Although she only served the company for five years, *Kanguk* (her name means "snow goose") has a guaranteed place in history as the last of a long line of HBC ships that started with the little ketch *Nonsuch* over three centuries before.

By 1987, the HBC was deep in debt. To help cut costs, it sold its 178 northern stores, its fur-auction houses and, although relatively insignificant in value, its last ship, among other assets. It was inevitable that the HBC would get out of the sea-freight business. The North was changing, as was the transportation of cargo to its remote outposts. Businesses were in a hurry; no one in the Arctic and subarctic wanted to wait from one summer to the next to receive supplies. Almost every settlement in the Canadian north had airstrips and was accessible for most of the year. Aviation was efficient and reliable. On land, a similar situation prevailed. With the vast improvement in Canada's road system over the decades, truck routes reached out from major hubs like spiderwebs. By 1987, almost nowhere in Canada, including its Arctic territories, was beyond reach year round of some form of transportation that was more efficient than the sea.

The HBC house flag, a British Red Ensign with the company's initial letters in white on the lower right quadrant, no longer flutters with pride from the masthead of ships navigating through drifting pack ice, and that in itself is sad. However, today there are marine shipping companies operating in the Arctic and the subarctic of Hudson Bay each open-water season. They are not affiliated to the HBC, but they do owe a huge debt to the organization that paved the way for them over the centuries by providing continually updated nautical charts and a massive library of literature on all aspects of the maritime history of the North. The intrepid captains and crews of the once-proud HBC fur-trade fleet were sailors of courage and dedication. And many of them, especially in the early days, were fine explorers. Most are long gone now, but it must be hoped that their history will never be forgotten. To that purpose, the HBC Archives in Winnipeg is a national treasure of untold importance.

Selected Bibliography

Beattie, Judith Hudson and Helen M. Buss. *Undelivered Letters to Hudson's Bay Company Men on the Northwest Coast of America, 1830–57.* Vancouver: UBC Press, 2003.

Dalton, Anthony. *Arctic Naturalist: The Life of J. Dewey Soper.* Toronto: Dundurn Press, 2010.

———. *Baychimo: Arctic Ghost Ship.* Victoria: Heritage House, 2006.

———. *The Graveyard of the Pacific.* Victoria: Heritage House, 2010.

Delgado, James P. *Made for the Ice.* Vancouver: Vancouver Maritime Museum and Underwater Archaeological Society of British Columbia, 1997.

Gray, Doug. *R.M.S. Nascopie, Ship of the North.* Ottawa: The Golden Dog Press, 1997.

Grenfell, Sir Wilfrid. *The Story of a Labrador Doctor.* London: Hodder & Stoughton, 1925.

LaFleur, Claude, ed. *Pilot of Arctic Canada.* Vol. 1. 2nd ed. Ottawa: Canadian Hydrographic Service, 1970.

McGoogan, Ken. *Ancient Mariner.* Toronto: Phyllis Bruce Books, 2003.

Newman, Peter C. *Caesars of the Wilderness.* Toronto: Penguin Books, 1987.

———. *Company of Adventurers.* Toronto: Penguin Books, 1985.

———. *Empire of the Bay.* Toronto: Madison Press, 1989.

———. *Merchant Princes.* Toronto: Penguin Books, 1991.

Maurice, Edward Beauclerk. *The Last of the Gentlemen Adventurers.* London: Fourth Estate, 2004.

Ships' Records. Hudson's Bay Company Archives. Winnipeg.

Spencer, Charles. *Prince Rupert: The Last Cavalier.* London: Weidenfeld & Nicolson, 2007.

Thomson, George Malcolm. *The Search for the Northwest Passage.* New York: Macmillan, 1975.

Wild, Roland. *Arctic Command.* Toronto: Ryerson Press, 1955.

Index

137

Index

Acknowledgements

I have long been fascinated by the many-faceted history of the Hudson's Bay Company. I believe I have read almost every book written about the company. I have studied, rowed, paddled and sailed versions of the boats that made up its hard-working inland fleets. I have explored some of the largest rapid-strewn rivers that were the transportation highways of the fur-trade era. And I have read the logbooks of many of the eclectic variety of ships that gave the fur trade its all-important ocean transportation. My heartfelt thanks go to the authors of those books, the designers and builders of the ships and boats, and the crews who risked so much for the fur trade.

I come by my interest in the long history of the HBC's fur trade honestly. I was born in Gravesend, England, on the south bank of the Thames River estuary. On that busy historic waterway of barges, freighters, passenger liners and naval ships, I learned to love the sea, the myriad types of vessels that travel on its waters and the rivers that feed its vastness. Early in life, I learned that the first HBC ships, *Nonsuch* and *Eaglet*, sailed from Gravesend to Hudson Bay, as did so many that followed.

In the fall of 2010, I walked along Gravesend's waterfront, the first time I had done so for well over five decades. Stopping to soak in the once-familiar scenery, I glanced at the pebbly beach in front of me, glistening in the October sun, and the waters that washed the pebbles clean. Out on the river, a restless fleet of small boats rode to their anchors, straining against the cold wind that swept whitecaps upriver against the current. On the opposite bank, in the direction of London, I could see the outline of the once-proud and bustling Tilbury Docks. I closed my eyes, and my memory took me back to my boyhood when I went out

Acknowledgements

with my late uncle, a Thames River pilot, in his sleek wooden motorboat. As a result of my recent brief visit, I realized that I owed a huge debt to the city of Gravesend for my earliest nautical education and the beginnings of my interest in the fur-trade era.

In the mid-1970s, I spent much of a summer in and around Stromness, in the Orkney Islands, where I often talked with men who had served on ships operated by the HBC. I owe that lovely seaport, those wonderful old sailors and those beautiful northern islands a big thank you too.

In memoriam, I thank Percy W. Corby, my uncle, who lost his life in a tragic accident at Tilbury Docks in 1949, for first showing a wide-eyed young boy the wonders of the sea.

Among those who have made the journey of researching and writing this book so special, I must thank eminent underwater archaeologist and explorer James Delgado for sharing his knowledge over recent years. A special word of thanks goes to my friend and fellow writer Jill Butcher. In England, Jill helped me find childhood memories and made my research journey more vivid than I could have imagined. Closer to home, I am indebted to the staff of the Hudson's Bay Company Archives in Winnipeg for many years of assistance. At Heritage House, again, my thanks go to publisher Rodger Touchie for asking me to work on the company's *Amazing Stories* series, to managing editor Vivian Sinclair for her professionalism and understanding, and to my editor, Lesley Reynolds, for the pleasure of working with her.

About the Author

Anthony Dalton is the author of 10 non-fiction books and co-author of two others, many of which are about the sea, ships or boats. These include *Polar Bears*; *A Long, Dangerous Coastline*; *The Graveyard of the Pacific*; *Baychimo: Arctic Ghost Ship*; and *Alone Against the Arctic*, all published by Heritage House. He is past president of the Canadian Authors Association and is dedicated to the craft of writing. A former expedition leader working alternately in the Sahara and the Arctic, he divides his time between homes in Tsawwassen, BC, and the nearby Gulf Islands.

More Amazing Stories by Anthony Dalton

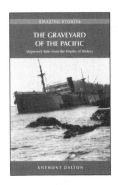

The Graveyard of the Pacific

Shipwreck Tales from the Depths of History

(ISBN 978-1-926613-31-4)

The magnificent west coast of Vancouver Island is renowned for its rugged splendour, but the coastline known as the Graveyard of the Pacific is haunted by the ghosts of doomed ships and long-dead mariners. These true tales of disastrous shipwrecks and daring rescues are a fascinating adventure into West Coast maritime history.

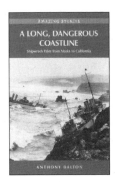

A Long, Dangerous Coastline

Shipwreck Tales from Alaska to California

(ISBN 978-1-926613-73-4)

From San Francisco's Golden Gate to the Inside Passage of British Columbia and Alaska, the west coast of North America has taken a deadly toll. Here are the dramatic tales of ships that met their end on this treacherous coastline— including *Princess Sophia*, *Queen of the North* and others—and the tragic stories of those who sailed aboard them.

Visit heritagehouse.ca to see the entire list of books in this series.

More Amazing Stories by Anthony Dalton

Polar Bears

The Arctic's Fearless
Great Wanderers

Anthony Dalton

(ISBN 978-1-926613-74-1)

Considered wise and powerful by the Inuit and other Native cultures, and celebrated in legend and literature, polar bears have become a charismatic symbol of animals threatened by climate change in the Arctic ecosystem. Yet for centuries, polar bears were demonized and slaughtered by adventurers who sailed the icy seas seeking wealth and glory. These fascinating stories from northern lands, including Canada, Alaska, Greenland and the Norwegian islands of Spitsbergen, draw from the annals of Arctic exploration and more recent polar bear research to capture the ingenuity, power and majesty of the world's largest land carnivore.

Visit www.heritagehouse.ca to see the entire list of books in this series.